Celebrating with
St. Joseph Altars

THE SOUTHERN TABLE

Cynthia LeJeune Nobles, Series Editor

IHS
IHS

Celebrating with St. Joseph Altars

The History, Recipes, and Symbols of a New Orleans Tradition

SANDRA SCALISE JUNEAU

LOUISIANA STATE UNIVERSITY PRESS
BATON ROUGE

Published by Louisiana State University Press
lsupress.org

Manufactured in the United States of America
Third printing, 2025

Unless otherwise stated, all photographs are by the author.

Designer: Barbara Neely Bourgoyne
Typefaces: Sina Nova, text; Scotch, display
Printer and binder: Versa Press

Cover and title page photo: St. Joseph's Altar at St. Francis Xavier Church in Metairie, Louisiana. Photo by Anthony "Chopper" Leone.

Library of Congress Cataloging-in-Publication Data
Names: Juneau, Sandra Scalise, author.
Title: Celebrating with St. Joseph altars : the history, recipes, and symbols of a New Orleans tradition / Sandra Scalise Juneau.
Description: Baton Rouge : Louisiana State University Press, [2021] | Series: The Southern table | Includes index.
Identifiers: LCCN 2020041880 | ISBN 978-0-8071-7476-0 (cloth)
Subjects: LCSH: Saint Joseph's Day—Louisiana—New Orleans Region. | Catholic Church—Customs and practices. | Cooking, Italian—Sicilian style. | LCGFT: Cookbooks.
Classification: LCC GT4995.J66 J96 2021 | DDC 392.3/7—dc23
LC record available at https://lccn.loc.gov/2020041880

To St. Joseph, for bringing together family, friends, and neighbors in a true spirit of community, that he may bless all those who lovingly work in his honor.

With gratitude for those past generations who nurtured and shared this sacred heritage, may they rest with the angels.

To all who participate in this tradition, may they be filled with *abbondanza,* the abundance of blessings that the St. Joseph Altar tradition cultivates.

Contents

Foreword

The celebration of the St. Joseph Altar is a deep-rooted tradition in New Orleans brought by the Italians from Sicily. In the Middle Ages, the people of Sicily were experiencing a drought. They prayed through the intercession of St. Joseph and promised that, if the drought ended, they would honor him yearly and thank him for his prayers on their behalf.

This book was written by Sandra Scalise Juneau, a native New Orleanian. She had two Sicilian-born grandmothers who taught her about food as art and love. The message that she shares through this work is what she has learned about the sacred tradition of St. Joseph Altars. She has gathered information from family members and many others in order to further explain the custom of preparing and visiting St. Joseph Altars as one of promise, petition, and thanksgiving.

Her reflections are written from a family perspective in which she traces the history, religious symbolism, and significance of the tradition from its Sicilian beginnings. She then moves into today's multicultural celebration and gives detailed suggestions for creating the St. Joseph Altar at home or for the public.

Included in her introspections are centuries-old recipes gathered from family and friends, and they include Sicilian confections and savory dishes customarily served at St. Joseph Altars. The photographs she presents go back to the 1930s and help the reader get in touch with this great New Orleans tradition.

Her hope, as well as mine, is that as you read this book you will be drawn not only to know more about the St. Joseph Altar, but to more deeply appreciate the rich tradition and generous spirit of hospitality it embodies.

—ARCHBISHOP GREGORY M. AYMOND
Archdiocese of New Orleans

Preface

Having been nurtured in a Sicilian-Louisianan family that took part in continuous celebrations, and for lagniappe, having two Sicilian-born grandmothers who taught me about food as art and love, I am happy to share the intricacies of the rich St. Joseph Altar tradition. The annual ritual includes recipes, prescribed methods, lore, and religious symbolism passed down through countless generations. It is my privilege to offer the story of this sacred heritage to you, and by writing this book I hope to help sustain this cultural treasure.

There was a time between the latter 1960s and into the 1980s when the preparation of St. Joseph Altars seemed to be dying out. After the passing of those Sicilian immigrants who came to New Orleans around the turn of the twentieth century and who brought the tradition to us, I, like so many of Sicilian heritage, thought all would be forever lost. But over the years I have given lectures and classes on the topic, and many individuals and groups have shown enthusiastic interest. In particular, I am always delighted by the curiosity of those learning about the altar for the first time.

Today, the preparation of the altar has seen a resurgence. Most encouraging, beyond being a Roman Catholic practice of Sicilian origin, the St. Joseph Altar celebration has become multicultural, embraced today by Catholics of African, Asian, and Hispanic heritage, as well as by Anglicans, Lutherans, and other religious groups. Younger generations have also revived the tradition, and because of this new interest I am hopeful that the custom will not only continue, but will flourish with a new spirit of devotion.

While preparations for St. Joseph Altars have adapted to local ingredients and tastes, most of the traditional dishes still follow cooking and baking methods that have been virtually unchanged for centuries. Unfortunately, for countless families of Sicilian heritage, many treasured St. Joseph Altar recipes have been lost to posterity. For others, written recipes that survived for generations were washed away in the 2005 floods of Hurricane Katrina.

Though I had been gathering family recipes since the mid-1960s, in the aftermath of Hurricane Katrina it became my mission to seek out recipes and preparation methods from friends in an effort to document those that otherwise might have vanished. Researching and restoring lost recipes was, for me, like breathing life again into treasured family traditions. Looking for these recipes required long hours of interviewing individuals and groups. I was typically greeted with enthusiasm, and I felt a spiritual connection with everyone I encountered.

Even though few written recipes or preparation methods for St. Joseph Altar specialties had survived, traditions continued in annual repetition, passed along orally from family to family. Most often, original recipes, particularly for confections, were in huge proportions suitable for a St. Joseph Altar production. To make sure these recipes would pass the tests of taste and time, I prepared them in my home kitchen with scaled-down quantities of ingredients.

One of the first lessons I learned when seeking out recipes was that very rarely will you receive recipes from different sources that are exactly alike. Family recipes for any of the traditional Sicilian favorites usually vary with individual interpretation, often with subtle distinctions of ingredients and cooking methods.

What I have assembled in this book are family recipes that have come down to me through the generations. I have also included treasured family recipes graciously shared by friends. Because I firmly believe that a recipe should be just a guideline, I do encourage you to make these dishes your own, possibly by adding a flavoring or changing the method to what is most familiar to you.

For this or any cookbook, before preparing a recipe the first step is to take the time to read the list of ingredients and the preparation method. Next, assemble all ingredients and equipment. Finally, read the recipe again to be sure you are familiar with the ingredients and cooking directions.

Large St. Joseph Altars require many hours of baking. Extended families and volunteers usually do the necessary preparation, often working in school kitchens or in commercial bakeries. Most ancient cultures practiced the act of communal baking, whether of foods for sustenance, such as bread, or in the preparation of celebratory sweets. Those shared culinary celebrations fostered spiritual connections within communities, as it still does when groups work to put together a St. Joseph Altar. Certainly, you would find it a joy to walk into any kitchen in the process of rolling, cutting, baking, and icing countless assorted cookies. But the best feeling to strike you would be the warmth of camaraderie.

Baking together has a magical way of forging friendships and bridging generations, as questions about family often lead to stories from family lore. When you visit a St. Joseph Altar, you will encounter age-old customs brought alive through the work of many hands. An altar assemblage is presented on heirloom linens and is decorated with flowers and candles. The feast for sharing features cakes, assorted cookies, vegetables, and specialty foods, all presented with exquisite artistry. The various elements found on St. Joseph Altars, including the food, contain symbolism. As you read about these symbols, I hope you gain an understanding of the significance that each individual item represents.

It is my wish that you will behold this splendor in communion with the loving spirit of generosity that each altar offers. And may you share in *abbondanza,* the abundance of blessings that comes from participation in the St. Joseph Altar tradition.

SAINT
JOSEPH
FAVA BEAN
ROSARY

Celebrating with St. Joseph Altars

Making *cuccidati* at the home of Angelina Caronna Accardo (*seated far right*), New Orleans, ca. 1955. Photo by P. H. Guarisco, courtesy of the author.

1

The History of St. Joseph Altars

Promise, Petition, Thanksgiving

When I was growing up in New Orleans in the 1940s, right after each Christmas my Sicilian-born maternal grandmother, Angelina Caronna Accardo, whom we called Mommie, would begin organizing and assembling her crew for "Making the Altar." With friends committed to help, she scheduled baking and cooking dates and solicited donations for supplies. The following weeks would be filled with endless hours of preparation for la Festa di San Giuseppe, the Feast of St. Joseph, celebrated annually on the nineteenth of March.

Mommie Accardo was carrying on a tradition celebrated in her home village of Poggioreale, Sicily, from as far back as perhaps the twelfth century. Beliefs held since earliest Christianity tell that St. Joseph, spouse of Mary and foster father of the Child Jesus, was graced with the gifts of obedience, faithfulness, patience, and justice. As Protezione della Famiglia Santa, or Protector of the Holy Family, St. Joseph was revered for his example of blessedness. Celebrated as the embodiment of goodness, he became the spiritual model for the faithful Sicilians to follow.

Since its inception, the tradition of making St. Joseph Altars has been constantly celebrated, despite famine, wars, and cultural displacement. Today still, through good times and bad, this communal practice brings families and neighbors together and sustains them with a shared spirituality. Through it all, generations have paid tribute to St. Joseph with a trilogy of resolves.

First, there is the promise. This is a sacred pledge made to St. Joseph to honor his feast day with a display of specially prepared foods, all to be shared in a collective banquet. Often this promise is renewed from generation to generation.

Second, there is petition. In times of need, such as illness, wars, and drought, devout Sicilians have offered the making of St. Joseph Altars as prayers of petition, asking for the intercession of St. Joseph to fulfill their requests.

Finally, there is thanksgiving. The making of St. Joseph Altars is a way of paying homage to St. Joseph, to give thanks for many blessings received. The St. Joseph Feast is shared by all, and even visitors to a St. Joseph Altar partake of the protection, hospitality, and love for which St. Joseph is revered.

Beloved Sicily

The story of the St. Joseph Altar is interwoven with both abundance and deprivation, and it begins with a great famine that devastated the entire island of Sicily. But before the magnitude of this tragedy can be comprehended, there must be a true appreciation of the Sicilian spirit—of tenacity, of connectedness to the land, and of reverence for blessings bestowed over the centuries.

Renowned as an isle of abundance, Sicily is endowed with seasons of nature's bounty, gifts that spring from her soil and are gathered from her surrounding seas. The scent of wild anise covers her hills in springtime. The warming summer sun sweetens her vines laden with grapes. Since ancient times, Phoenicians and Greeks were drawn to this island of plenty. In *The Odyssey,* Homer's epic poem of ancient Greece, his hero, Odysseus, describes an orchard in Sicilia:

> . . . four spacious acres planted
> with trees in bloom or weighted down for picking:
> pear trees, pomegranates, brilliant apples,
> luscious figs, and olives ripe and dark.
> Fruit never failed upon these trees: winter
> and summer time they bore, for through the year

the breathing Westwind ripened all in turn—
one pear came to prime, and then another,
and so with apples, figs, and the vine's fruit
empurpled in the royal vineyard there.
Currants were dried at one end, on a platform
bare to the sun, beyond the vintage arbors
and vats the vintners trod; while near at hand
were new grapes barely formed as the green bloom fell,
or half-ripe clusters, faintly coloring.
After the vines came rows of vegetables
of all the kinds that flourish in every season,
and through the garden plots and orchard ran
channels from one clear fountain, while another
gushed through a pipe under the courtyard entrance
to serve the house and all who came for water.

When Paul of Tarsus visited Syracuse around AD 59, Sicily had already been enriched by Phoenician, Carthaginian, Greek, Roman, and Jewish cultures. St. Paul's message of faith, hope, and love united Sicilians with Christ's teachings. Christianity quickly spread, taking root as Sicily's most influential creed. Many shrines of Christian saints dot the island, and today, still, their memories are celebrated with religious traditions.

One of the earliest Christians was Lucia of Syracuse. Legends tell of Lucia, a young woman of nobility whose family had arranged for her marriage. Steadfast in devotion to her Christian beliefs, Lucia, whose name means light, had dedicated her life to Christ. Although she was betrothed, she declined to marry and vowed to remain a virgin. Her betrothed was not a Christian, and he became so enraged by her refusal that he arranged for Lucia's capture and ordered her death. Since AD 304, devotions to Santa Lucia, the virgin-martyr, have generated sacred memorials in Sicily and throughout Christianity. Often portrayed in Christian art holding a plate with her eyes, signifying the legend of her brutal death, St. Lucy is known for the light of her faith. As the patron saint for those with eye illnesses, she is usually honored on St. Joseph Altars with a *cuccidata,* a decorative fig cake depicting St. Lucy's plate, or with a bowl of salted chickpeas called *cecida,* which represent the Occhi di Santa Lucia, or Eyes of St. Lucy. The Feast of St. Lucy, commemorated annually on the thirteenth of December, is often celebrated with a special dish in her honor, a sweet custard of whole-wheat berries cooked with honey, called *cuccia*.

Since antiquity, wheat has grown in Sicilia in such abundance that the island is known as "the granary of Rome." Prized for its strategic location, this land of plenty was ruled by a changing parade of controlling nations, each successive conquering group endowing the island with gifts from their culture. The Saracens, for instance, planted eggplants, almonds, lemons, and oranges. They also cultivated sugarcane and rice, and introduced such exotic spices as cinnamon, pepper, nutmeg, and clove. Sicilians thankfully accepted those luxuriant gifts and celebrated them through a repetition of liturgical traditions that strengthened their Christian faith.

Since the Middle Ages, Sicily's fertile land was controlled by large feudal estates. The peasant population was governed by rules imposed by the Vandals, the Byzantines, the Angevins, the Normans, the Spanish, and the French. Yet throughout their long history of foreign conquest, the Sicilian spirit endured.

Holding to their religious traditions, the Sicilian faithful had adopted San Giuseppe, St. Joseph, as their patron, seeking his intercession during times of need. From stories passed down orally from generation to generation, it is believed that sometime around the twelfth century Sicily experienced a lengthy, catastrophic drought. Wheat stalks withered, crops failed, cattle died, and people were starving, so Sicilians directed their prayers of petition to St. Joseph, asking la Protezione della Famiglia Santa for relief. In return, they promised to honor St. Joseph in commemoration of his feast day.

Their faith never wavered, and by this trust in Divine Providence they were sustained through the drought. As legend tells, salvation came in the form of the lowly but hardy fava bean. Favas, often used as fodder for cattle, were able to survive and grow in the parched earth. This was the starving Sicilians' lifesaving crop, and the fava bean became a symbol of their hope.

When the rains finally returned, the faithful fulfilled their promise, gathering their meager foods to share in a feast of thanksgiving in honor of their patron, St. Joseph. From this humble beginning, the St. Joseph Altar tradition flourished. Throughout Sicily, la Festa di San Giuseppe became a celebration of the blessings of the earth, with each village creating its own unique customs. In the typically generous and creative spirit of Sicilians, everyone shared in the feast. Soon, the single day of thanksgiving grew into a festival with many days of celebration, combining sacred devotion with culinary artistry, music, and pageantry.

At these festivals, simple peasant foods were presented with creative flair, offering a means of nourishing Sicilians' sense of beauty and telling the story of their beliefs and heritage. Each loaf of bread, for example, was fashioned into a fanciful shape, representing different religious symbols from Christian lore. Sicily's love affair with sugar inspired endless varieties of sweets, including assorted biscotti in flavors such as almond, anise, chocolate, cinnamon, clove, and lemon. There were also the classic sweetened ricotta and custard-filled confections of cannoli, *cassateda,* and *sfinge di San Giuseppe.* With each family laboring to surpass the culinary artistry of their neighbors, the displays eventually took on an air of competition.

Each St. Joseph Altar was unique, a devotional display reflecting each family's distinctive creativity. The tables that held this bounty were dressed in the finest linens, cherished hand-stitched lace and embroidered cloths bequeathed *dalla nonna alla figlia,* from grandmother to daughter. In celebration of springtime's gifts, the altars were filled with bounteous displays of vegetables, fruit, and flowers. Finally, there were candles, each representing a petition or favor asked of St. Joseph. With all the varied food elements brought together, the St. Joseph Altars represented *abbondanza,* the abundance of faith, hope, and love with which the devout Sicilians had been blessed.

St. Joseph Altars in Louisiana

By the end of the nineteenth century, absentee landlords controlled over two-thirds of the farmlands in Sicily, affording the huge peasant class no chance of upward mobility. Neither the unfulfilled promises of General Garibaldi, one of Italy's "fathers of the fatherland," nor his 1860 efforts in unification improved living conditions for Sicilians. For this reason, between 1880 and 1915, approximately four million Italians, mostly from Sicily, migrated to the United States.

The late nineteenth through early twentieth century waves of Sicilian immigration brought the St. Joseph Altar tradition to Louisiana. Drawn to a similar climate and recruited as workers for sugarcane plantations, the majority of migrant Sicilians settled in south Louisiana. They came from the fruit-growing regions of Sicily, mostly from the towns of Bisacquino, Caccamo, Cefalu, Chiusa Sclafani, Contessa Entellina, Corleone, Gibellina, Palazzo Adriano, Palermo, Poggioreale, Piana dei Greci, Roccamena, Salaparuta, Sambuca, Termini, Trabia, and Trapani, and from the island of Ustica. They arrived with little more than their hopes for a better life, along with the blessings of their rich cultural heritage: a strong work ethic; their creativity, especially through food as art; their strong sense of family; and, like their ancestors, the sustaining gift of their religious faith.

Despite the strange English and French languages and customs they encountered upon arrival in New Orleans, Sicilian immigrants thrived. In particular, they seized the opportunities afforded them in the fertile soils of southeast Louisiana's farmlands, and they became leaders in growing and selling produce. In their new homeland, wherever they settled their families, they gave thanks, each year honoring St. Joseph for their many blessings. Communal preparations for St. Joseph Altars gave these immigrant families an unbroken connection to their ancestral heritage. From family to family, they found the comfort of continuity in a sacred tradition that nourished their souls.

The earliest St. Joseph Altars in Louisiana were set up in the "front rooms," or living rooms, of homes in the neighborhoods of New Orleans, the Westbank, and Kenner, and in St. Bernard, Jefferson, and Tangipahoa parishes. Without fail, the arrival of springtime in South Louisiana was celebrated each year with la Tavola di San Giuseppe, the Table of St. Joseph. By the 1920s, the St. Joseph's Day Feast had become firmly established among Louisiana's many celebrations. St. Joseph Altars appeared in storefronts and even in restaurants run by Sicilian families in the French Quarter of New Orleans. Guests were invited to share in the feasts, often through public notices placed in local newspapers.

Throughout the first half of the twentieth century, most of Louisiana's St. Joseph Altars were held in homes. At this time, welcoming family and friends into the average house required weeks of preparation with the help of countless volunteers, all working within the limitations of family-sized kitchens. Often whole families helped clear the front room to make space for the altar and to open up a walking path for a flow of visitors. In the backyard would be arrangements of tables assembled for seating guests to share in the delectable St. Joseph's Day Feast. Each guest would be served a platter that included copious portions of the traditional *pasta con le sarde,* pasta with anise and sauced with a sardine- or anchovy-flavored tomato gravy, always topped with seasoned bread crumbs called *mudica*. The pasta would be served with assorted vegetable omelets called *froscia,* bread, wine, and endless varieties of delicious sweets and biscotti.

Wartime Altars

During the war years of the 1940s, many families made altars in promise to St. Joseph as a prayer of petition for the protection of husbands, fathers, and sons who were away at war. In the years right after the war, I recall "Making the Nine Altars," a ritual of visiting nine St. Joseph Altars on the feast day. Our family's annual novena in tribute to St. Joseph began at my grandparents' home above their New Orleans grocery store on the corner of Clio and Liberty streets. We progressed to nine individual St. Joseph Altars, all within easy walking distance in their inner-city neighborhood. Each one we visited was distinctive. Each reflected the family's individuality, through displays of specialty baked breads and the fig-filled cookies called *cuccidati,* along with adornments of antique hand-embroidered linens, and often with treasured family photographs. All of those altars were unified by their shared ancient tradition, a legacy of tribute to their beloved San Giuseppe.

During one of those novenas I vividly remember seeing heart-shaped medals hanging beneath crossed palm fronds on windows and in doorways. The medals had gold borders and hung on purple ribbons. I knew the crossed palms indicated homes hosting St. Joseph Altars. My mother explained that the medals signified patriotic pride, and they were the military decorations known as Purple Hearts. Their display in windows signified that during the war a family member in that home had been injured or had given his life for our country.

Inside, on three-tiered altars laden with food, next to lighted candles and tucked in between bouquets of flowers would be framed photographs bordered in black. These were the pictures of good-looking soldiers in their starched, unblemished uniforms, their smiling faces forever fixed in timeless youth.

Like most St. Joseph Altars, the living rooms of homes displaying Purple Hearts were filled with the aromas of assorted biscotti, fresh flowers, and fruit. Among the comforting sights were clusters of mothers, widows, grandmothers, sisters, and aunts dressed in ritual black who hovered in smothering sadness. I will never forget these images of mourning for the loss of their boys.

In the long years following the end of the war, promises were continually kept with the making of annual St. Joseph Altars. Even today, many altars still display photographs of young soldiers who gave their lives for our country, not only from World War II, but from all the wars and conflicts since. For those blessed with safe return, many altars have been prepared with the help of husbands, fathers, and sons who came to appreciate the special protection that had been bestowed on them by St. Joseph.

St. Joseph Altar at the Convent of the Good Shepherd, New Orleans, Louisiana, ca. 1946.

The author gathers with her Scalise-Juneau family for a Table of St. Joseph in Metairie, Louisiana, 1978.

After World War II, some homes were unable to accommodate the overflow of visitors to their St. Joseph Altars. Many religious institutions then opened their doors, which provided grander spaces and which spread devotion to St. Joseph into a broader community.

In the past several decades, the universal appeal of the St. Joseph Altar tradition has transcended its uniquely Sicilian beginnings into celebrations with multicultural influences. In Louisiana, St. Joseph Altars can be found within African American, Hispanic, and Asian communities. Each group expresses its own cultural artistry, with identifying markers of individual heritage.

Just as Sicilian immigrants took this beloved tradition to their "new land," younger generations who have moved away from Louisiana have taken St. Joseph Altars with them wherever they have settled. Today, this prayer of thanksgiving to St. Joseph not only flourishes with impressive displays in Sicily and Louisiana, but also in cities and small communities across America, as well as in Canada, Mexico, and Australia.

Whether at small family celebrations in private homes or at elaborate St. Joseph Altars in churches or institutions, this tradition continues to bring together a diverse gathering to share in the bounty of St. Joseph's legacy, all in a loving way. For each individual—as a host of a St. Joseph Altar, as a volunteer helping with preparations, or just as a visitor—there is joy of participation in this ancient cultural treasure. A St. Joseph Altar overflows with generosity. As you visit one and behold these artistic displays, may they not only delight your culinary senses but also touch your soul with the true spirit of benevolence.

2

Making the Altar

Creating an altar shows reverence for St. Joseph's role as the Protector of the Holy Family, and this is always a special privilege. During this celebration of faith and devotion, guests are welcomed to partake in the Christian ceremonial breaking of bread. The table is the spiritual center of the tradition, and around it comes together a community of family, friends, and neighbors. As host, you play a vital role in gathering your community to this table of renewal.

Aside from the spiritual aspect, a St. Joseph Altar is a feast of culinary artistry, showcasing the finest that each individual, family, or devotional group can provide. No two St. Joseph Altars are ever alike. Each is a unique exhibition of individual creativity lovingly handcrafted and displayed with reverence.

This form of folk art is as distinct in design as individual Christmas trees. Most St. Joseph Altars, however, follow basic age-old customs, such as setting up the display in at least three tiers or steps, a tradition symbolizing the Holy Family—Gesù, Maria, e San Giuseppe; Jesus, Mary, and St. Joseph. In addition, you must make space for the traditional meal known as the "Feeding of the Saints," which occurs directly after the "Blessing of the Altar." (For "Blessing of the Altar" prayers, see appendix A.) The meal is served to the officiating priest and to participants who represent the Holy Family and saints who have taken part in your *Tupa-Tupa* pageant, the ritualistic "knocking on three doors."

When planning for a St. Joseph Altar in your home, you may also envision a small Table of St. Joseph, with just a few breads and cookies, possibly followed by a family meal of the traditional St. Joseph's Day specialties of *pasta con le sarde,* assorted vegetable *froscia,* and traditional Sicilian confections.

These few steps are probably the easiest way to begin. But I will caution you in advance. From my experience, once the word is out about your planned St. Joseph Altar, it will grow beyond your expectations. Friends, family, and even perfect strangers will offer help or just show up with specialties of baked goods, cooked foods, and their suggestions for setting up the altar. It will seem that St. Joseph has somehow taken over, and your altar will take on a life of its own. Take these gestures as a compliment. This spirit of generosity that surrounds St. Joseph Altars is all part of the tradition of the *abbondanza*.

Preparations

Opening your home for a St. Joseph Altar comes with the understanding that the altar you are about to create reaffirms holy tradition with the trilogy of faith, hope, and love, and that all are invited to participate in spiritual unity with the Holy Family. Putting the event together does require countless hours of work, and this labor of love is always more about the love than the labor. To assure a successful experience, it helps to have a little forethought and a lot of organization. Here are the steps to consider:

1. Event Date—Determine the date for your St. Joseph Altar. Although St. Joseph's feast day is March 19, for convenience many celebrations are held on the weekends right before or after that date. Traditionally the feast is held over two days, but again it is up to you to decide if you want to host your St. Joseph Altar on a single day or over two days.

2. Your Church Calendar—As soon as you have made the commitment to host a St. Joseph Altar, contact your local church parish priest to schedule a date and time for the Blessing of the Altar. The earlier you make this request, the better the chance of having your selected date and time available.

3. Public or Private—Decide if you want a private affair, for family and invited guests only, or if your St. Joseph Altar will be open to the public. Again, either way, your celebration can be as small or as elaborate as you wish.

4. Volunteers—As soon as you have made the above decisions, contact your volunteers. Whether working in a commercial bakery, church cafeteria, or your home kitchen, you will be welcoming into your heart a loving group of people dedicated to honoring the Feast of St. Joseph. Managing these willing helpers, however, takes strategy and organization.

5. Saints—Decide who will represent the saints for your St. Joseph Altar. Among the most cherished traditions of the altar is the representation of saints who participate in the *Tupa-Tupa* pageant, which culminates in the Feeding of the Saints ritual. (For more on the *Tupa-Tupa,* see chapter 3.) Usually the trilogy—Jesus, Mary, and Joseph—are represented by children or grandchildren of the hosting family. For some St. Joseph Altars, as many as a dozen saints are represented, sometimes by adult members of the community. It's up to you to choose the number of saints, and whether they should dress in period costume, a way of enhancing the drama of the pageant. Invitations to portray a saint should be extended as early as possible. Also determine where the pageant will be held, in your home or outdoors, and give some thought to which three doors participants will use.

6. Budget—Once you have determined your event's location, create a budget. Among the many traditions surrounding St. Joseph Altars is the belief that, as an act of humility, all supplies for the altar should be acquired by begging. Some hosts, however, personally buy whatever is needed and willingly accept donations of supplies or prepared foods. Depending on how you proceed, you will need to set up guidelines for expected costs. For future reference it helps to keep a log of supplies needed, costs, donations, vendors, and volunteers. It is almost guaranteed that, after you host your first St. Joseph Altar, you or a family member or friend who worked on your altar will continue in the following years. Your log will become a valuable tool for keeping the tradition alive.

7. Altar Placement—For either a home Table of St. Joseph or for a public St. Joseph Altar, determine where you will set up your display, always

allowing for possible expansion. When designing the layout for your altar placement, consider traffic flow, and make room for guests to easily enter and exit. Consider whether you will serve the traditional St. Joseph's Day meal (see appendix B for a sample menu). If so, you will need additional space away from the altar display for seating and serving guests. You must also plan to provide for automobile parking, perhaps with permission from neighbors for the use of their driveways. If you anticipate a large gathering, you might need to secure a special parking permit from local law enforcement.

8. Food Preparation—Schedule dates for baking and cooking months in advance, and make sure your volunteers have work dates and deadlines on their calendars. Bake the most durable cookies a few months ahead and store or freeze them. Plan to bake the most fragile cookies and cakes in the weeks and days just prior to March 19. Savory cooked foods should be prepared only days before serving, unless they are precooked and frozen until needed.

9. Order Early—Order and gather baking supplies as soon as possible. Usually baking begins just after Christmas, so nonperishable supplies should be ordered by mid-December. Of particular concern are dried figs for decorative *cuccidati*. The best figs for this purpose are those imported from Greece or Turkey and are usually packaged in rolls of fourteen-ounce packets, with twenty-four packets to a case. They can be ordered from local specialty-food wholesalers. Prices vary, and they are usually less expensive when purchased by the case, so you might consider purchasing a full case to split with friends and family. Dried figs are durable and will last several months if kept in a cool dry place. Just be sure to get your order in early.

   If you plan to use decorative breads from commercial bakeries, orders should be placed no later than early January. Also, it's not too early in January to preorder fresh fruit and specialty produce, such as artichokes, fresh anise, dried fava beans, and cardoons (*carduni*), all for a mid-March delivery.

The most commonly used nonperishables are flour, allspice, cinnamon, cloves, nutmeg, the pure extracts of anise, almond, lemon, and vanilla, granulated and powdered sugar, lard, vegetable shortening, canned milk, sesame seeds, almonds, pecans, and walnuts. Perishable ingredients such as eggs and fresh milk should not be purchased until ready for use.

Sources for Purchasing Specialty Supplies (including imported figs)

Acquistapace's Supermarket
125 E. 21st Ave.
Covington, LA 70433
phone 985-893-0593

Dorignac's Food Center
710 Veterans Blvd.
Metairie, LA 70005
phone 504-834-8216
email: info@dorignacs.com

Nor Joe's Imports
505 Frisco Ave.
Metairie, LA 70005
phone 504-833-9240
email: norjoeadm@gmail.com

Perrone & Sons, LLC Importers
1801 L and A Rd.
Metairie, LA 70001
phone 504-455-3663
email: info@perroneandsons.com

10. Flowers—Order flowers in January for a mid-March delivery. Traditionally, two identical bouquets of flowers are placed on the top altar tier beside the statue or image of St. Joseph. The lily, symbol of St. Joseph's purity, is usually included in the bouquet. Your choice of additional flowers will set the tone for your altar. An especially elegant display is one of all white flowers mixed with assorted greenery, though you may decide on a combination of pastel flowers or a mix of vibrantly colored flowers. Many of Louisiana's St. Joseph Altars feature varieties of red-striped amaryllis, known locally as St. Joseph Lilies, which are in their early springtime bloom during March.

St. Joseph Lilies.

11. Serving Pieces—As early as possible, begin gathering from family and friends a variety of candelabra, vases, punch bowls, and crystal dishes. You'll need these items to display the candles, flowers, fruit, vegetables, and assorted cookies that will embellish your altar. It helps to attach an identifying sticker to the bottom of each borrowed item for efficient return after you take down your altar.

12. Advertising—Once your initial organization is in place, consider how you will publicize your St. Joseph Altar. For a home *tavola,* you may send invitations by mail or email to family and friends. For a public display, contact your local newspapers and diocesan publication and give them information about your altar's time and location. Online news

sources are increasingly popular for advertising altars. In 2019, for example, wwltv.com listed over fifty locations in the New Orleans area for St. Joseph Altars open to the public. Be sure to include the time for the blessing and whether you will be serving the St. Joseph Feast to the public.

13. Sharing the Food—Plan ahead for the distribution of the foods displayed on the altar. For most private St. Joseph Altars, these foods are shared with family, volunteers, and invited guests. For most public St. Joseph Altars, a special meal is prepared for serving to visitors. "Breaking the altar" typically occurs after the viewing of public St. Joseph Altars is concluded, when nonperishable foods, cookies, and cakes are packaged and distributed to individuals and charitable organizations.

Setting the Table

ALTAR LOGISTICS

Determine the overall height of your altar, taking into account the ceiling height of the room. To give balance and proper perspective, an image of St. Joseph should be the altar's central feature, allowing for visual framing with ample ceiling height and wall space on each side. If you use a painting or tapestry image of St. Joseph, it should be centered and hung just above the top tier. If you are using a statue, it should be placed in the center of the top tier, allowing space on each side for candles and flowers. The statue or image of St. Joseph should be measured to assure that it will be in proper proportion or scale to the altar. A statue or image that is too large will overwhelm the overall effect, just as a too small statue or image will get lost among the altar's many embellishments.

For an elaborate St. Joseph Altar open to the public, the room or space where the altar will be set up should determine the configuration. For most altars, three tiers, or steps, are placed atop a standard-height table. The number of tiers is a matter of individual choice, but most typically there are at least three. Some extravagant St. Joseph Altars are set up with the central, tiered altar flanked on each side by angled tables. Still others combine a central, tiered altar with several standard-height tables grouped into the shape of a cross.

Before you attempt to position the tables, it would be helpful to have a scale drawing of your room layout. This guide will also become a valuable resource for replicating future setups. If your St. Joseph Altar is open to the public, consider roping off the entire display. This allows an orderly flow of visitors to view it while discouraging them from touching the food.

GATHER YOUR TABLES

The base table used for a St. Joseph Altar is typically a standard-height dining table. The simplest setup is to place this main table horizontally against the wall that will become the altar's focal point. Top this base table with three or more tiers, or steps. Each tier is usually slightly narrower than the one it rests upon, with each of the tiers approximately twelve to fifteen inches in height. There is no limit to the number of tiers you can choose although traditionally there are at least three tiers over the tabletop level, for a total of four.

Each tier will be laden with breads, cookies, candles, and flowers. To avoid toppling, make certain the tiers are firmly secured in place. If you have ample storage space, a larger, permanent St. Joseph Altar can be built, and then stored for future use.

Plan to provide a separate dining table for the ceremonial Feeding of the Saints. This ritual meal is traditionally served after the Blessing of the Altar. Guests at this table will include the priest presiding over the blessing, along with the individuals representing saints. Your space will determine the placement of this table. For St. Joseph Altars held in large community settings, the "saints' table" is usually placed horizontally, several feet in front of the St. Joseph Altar. For a St. Joseph Altar held in a private home, it may be placed on either side of the altar, or it may be set in the dining room, away from the main altar. This special table is usually arranged elegantly, featuring your finest linens, china, crystal, and silverware, perhaps with a small floral arrangement and place cards identifying each of the saints represented.

Gift bags, St. Joseph Altar, AVO Restaurant, New Orleans.

Finally, consider providing a special table for holding gifts for your guests. Traditionally included are a prayer card and a holy medal, items that honor specific saints, along with a bit of bread, several sweet biscotti, and a "lucky bean," a roasted fava bean. All items should be blessed along with the ritual Blessing of the Altar, and it helps if they are packed ahead in small paper or cellophane bags. The biscotti are meant to be eaten, symbolizing the sharing in St. Joseph's hospitality. Because all the items are blessed, aside from the biscotti, they are often saved as sacred mementos, each with its own special meaning. In many homes, the blessed bread is saved and is sometimes tossed into the wind with a prayer for safety during hurricanes. The lucky bean often finds its way into pockets and purses as a prayer for abundance.

PLACEMENTS ON THE ALTAR

Once the main St. Joseph Altar is built and secured in place, it's time to dress it. Among the most stunning features of traditional St. Joseph Altars are the table linens. Just as your selection of linens sets the pace for a formal dinner, the selection of fine linens on your St. Joseph Altar will set the tone for the finesse of your display.

You will need two layers of tablecloths, preferably all white or off-white, and don't be shy about borrowing them from family or friends. The first layer should be plain white, possibly new bedsheets set aside for this purpose. Beginning with the bottom tier, pin the white cloths in place so that they cover the top, sides, and front of the altar. Next should come layers of decorative linens. This is where you can showcase antique lace or hand-stitched heirlooms. Drape the decorative linens over each step, laying them smoothly over the layer of plain white cloths. If your linens have ornamental edging, be sure these embellishments are displayed on the front of each tier. Reserve the finest linens for decorating the front of the bottom tier, which is the most visible part of the altar.

The top tier of the altar is traditionally dedicated to St. Joseph, and it holds a statue or image as the dominant focal point. The area around the statue is embellished with flowers, candles, and sometimes an arrangement of fresh palms.

The second tier, which is below the top, should display representations of Christ, possibly centered with cross-shaped bread, or with a *cuccidata* in the shape of a cross or of an ostensorium, also known as a monstrance, which is the vessel used to exhibit the Eucharist during Benediction of the Blessed Sacrament. Arrangements of fruit and vegetables could balance each side, possibly mounded into punch bowls. You can also place assorted bread shapes, such as the circle, symbolizing everlasting love, or the fish, symbolizing the early Christians. These breads, along with decorative bottles of wine are displayed to represent the Mystical Body and Blood of Christ.

The third tier is placed over the base tabletop, and it usually displays breads or *cuccidati* in shapes of the Sacred Heart to represent Mary and the staff to represent St. Joseph.

The tabletop level is where most of the cakes, cookies, and cooked foods will be placed. To complete an effect of abundance, you can add decorative cakes in various shapes, such as a bible, a lamb, or a heart. Add plates of varied flavored biscotti, *pignolati,* and lucky beans. Add color with mounds of lemons and oranges, and an assortment of fresh springtime vegetables such as anise, *carduni,* fava beans, and fennel. Other offerings might include a shallow bowl of *mudica,* the seasoned bread crumbs symbolizing the sawdust of St. Joseph's workshop. A bowl of *mudica* is usually embellished with three bay leaves to symbolize the Holy Family. You can include a bowl of salted chickpeas, called *cecida,* representing the Eyes of St. Lucy. This is also the proper location for plates of cooked foods, which often include stuffed artichokes, assorted vegetable *froscia,* baked and stuffed redfish, and in Louisiana, locally boiled crawfish or other shellfish.

To honor other saints, add small statues of their images and intersperse them with devotional candles, each candle representing a prayer of petition, thanksgiving, or remembrance.

Once assembled, your altar will become a celebration of *abbondanza,* and it will represent St. Joseph's hospitality. And since it is said that, "once St. Joseph gets hold of you, he rarely lets go," your spectacular work will hopefully encourage following generations to carry on the tradition.

St. Joseph Altar with rosary of candles, Convent of the Good Shepherd, 1975.

3

Tupa-Tupa

The *Tupa-Tupa* reenactment traditionally takes place immediately before the blessing of a St. Joseph Altar. The Sicilian word *tupa* means to knock, and this pageant tells the story of Bethlehem, when Joseph, protector of the Holy Family, was seeking shelter for Mary before the birth of Baby Jesus. Central to the theme of faith and trust in Divine Providence is the act of knocking on three doors by a procession of those portraying the Holy Family: Jesus, Mary, and Joseph. The participants can also include an accompaniment of many saints, and even angels.

The ritual has been associated with the St. Joseph Altar tradition in Sicily for many centuries. In some villages, it takes the form of a street procession, with bands of music and entire communities chanting traditional prayers in holy reverence. Any number of saints might be dressed in costumes. Typically, someone portrays Mary, who rides a donkey and is assisted by St. Joseph walking beside her. The procession continues through village streets as throngs of the faithful join in the sacred celebration. Street processions continue today in some Sicilian villages.

The Local Script

In Louisiana, St. Joseph Altars offer a less elaborate representation of the tradition. Those portraying saints might appear in period costume, or they might wear their Sunday best. Foregoing a street procession, the pageant is planned around approaches to three doors. If enacted outdoors, the saints knock on predesignated doors of houses along the procession to the altar. If the procession is held indoors, the saints knock on doors that open to different rooms within the building. Behind each door is a member of the cast who has rehearsed with ready answers.

At the first door, the person representing St. Joseph knocks and says, "We are seeking shelter. May we come in?" The answer is given through the closed door, "No, we have no room for you here."

At the second door, the person portraying St. Joseph again knocks and says, "We are weary from our long travels. Can we please spend the night here?" Again, through the closed door the answer is given, "No, we have no room for you here."

The procession moves to the third door. Again, St. Joseph knocks and asks, "From our long travels we are weary and we are seeking shelter. Can you please take us in?" The door is flung open with the words, "Welcome. Come in. The feast has been prepared for you."

The pageant continues as Jesus, Mary, Joseph, and any other saints or angels go inside to the St. Joseph Altar display. The presiding priest then blesses the St. Joseph Altar in a traditional ceremony.

Blessing of St. Joseph Altar at Our Lady of the Lake Catholic School, Mandeville, Louisiana, 1986. Reverend Monsignor Joseph L. Chotin performs the ceremony, with students portraying the saints and an angel.

Feeding of the Saints

After the Blessing of the Altar, the presiding priest is seated at a special dining table with those portraying the Holy Family and the other saints from the *Tupa-Tupa*. The Feeding of the Saints always begins with three types of fruit, usually orange and grapefruit, along with cherries or strawberries. Next, each participant in the pageant is served a small taste of the blessed foods on the altar, first a bit of fish, then a small portion of pasta, a taste of stuffed artichoke or other vegetable, and always bread. This is followed by an assortment of confections, possibly a taste of cannoli or of assorted sweet biscotti.

Tradition dictates that none of the food on the altar can be served to guests until after the saints have finished their meal. If the St. Joseph Altar is held in a private home, the feast is shared with all those present as soon as the Feeding of the Saints is completed. If the St. Joseph Altar is open for public display, the table for the saints is cleared after their meal, and the doors are then opened for viewing by visitors. At this time, some public St. Joseph Altars offer plates of the traditional feast to all visitors.

It's Up to You

As St. Joseph Altar traditions change, the sequence of events is open to individual interpretation. At some St. Joseph Altars, the Blessing of the Altar occurs on the evening before the Feast Day, with the *Tupa-Tupa* procession enacted the following morning. At others, the Blessing of the Altar occurs just after the *Tupa-Tupa* procession on the morning or afternoon of St. Joseph's Feast Day. In order to accommodate a greater number of visitors, St. Joseph Altars are now often held over the weekend that falls closest to March 19, a celebration that truly has become "a movable feast."

The blessing of a St. Joseph Altar itself has many different versions, and over the years some ceremonies have varied greatly. At some St. Joseph Altars, for example, the night before the Feast of St. Joseph is the time for the recitation of the Litany and Rosary of St. Joseph, immediately followed by the blessing. At others, the Litany and Rosary are recited the evening before, with the Blessing of the Altar performed the next morning, on St. Joseph's Feast Day.

Perseverance Pays

In explaining the significance of the *Tupa-Tupa* procession, my grandmother often reminded me, and I have repeated to my children that, whatever the challenge, "Don't give up at that first knock. If you have to, knock again. And if necessary, don't hesitate to knock that third time."

4

Becoming a Saint

I was only five years old. It was December 13, 1945, la Festa di Santa Lucia, the Feast of St. Lucy, just as I was savoring the luscious taste of honey drizzled over a bowl of warm *cuccia,* when my grandmother told me I was going to be a saint. I was excited and too young to realize that "sainthood" was selectively bestowed posthumously as a privilege of the virtuous deceased. I was also completely unaware of what I'd been chosen for, that among the many customs of St. Joseph Altars is the ceremonial ritual of having young children portray Jesus, Mary, and Joseph.

In my family, Lucia's Feast Day was always the time for our symbolic "lighting" of the Christmas Season. Honoring Lucia, whose name means "light," it was on this special night that we turned on our Christmas tree lights. Because my birthday falls in mid-December, just three days after the Feast of St. Lucy, for most of my young years I thought all of this celebration was just for me.

Aside from my birthday, this special day also signaled something else important—this was the beginning of an intense cooking and baking season. Our Sicilian–New Orleans family honored centuries of religious tradition with a seemingly endless progression of winter and early spring celebrations that all required food. Closing my eyes, I still recall sensations that envelop me with smells and tastes of preparations for the "Holy Days" that stretched from the Feast of St. Lucy in mid-December all the way through March 19, the Feast of St. Joseph.

My earliest reminiscences of this time of year are of delicious aromas. Whenever I encounter the flavor of anise, I am instantly transported on a wave of nostalgia back to the security of Mommie Accardo's kitchen warmth. For my fifth birthday that year and throughout that holiday season I basked in my specialness. But I also remember being mesmerized by my grandmother slowly melting sugar into a golden caramel, then tossing in hand-cut bits of fried pasta and coating each piece, which she quickly formed into pyramids or pine-cone shapes called *pignolati*. I loved watching her magically create delicious food, and it was only between her times at the stove that I allowed my mind to wander with visions of myself among the hosts of heavenly saints.

Christmas Eve is traditionally a day of abstinence from meat, and each year our family welcomed Gesù Bambino with a delectable supper of my grandmother's Sicilian-style oyster soup, served with *schiacciata,* a freshly baked pan bread infused with onions and anchovies. After Midnight Mass and before opening our presents we celebrated with warm nutmeg-spiced eggnog and a sumptuous feast that progressed from antipasto to ziti. On Christmas morning we awoke to the sizzling smells of homemade, anise-flavored sausage.

January 6 is King's Day, which ushers in the beginning of the New Orleans carnival season and a stream of parades. This holiday typically arrived with the scent of yeast bread spiced with cinnamon, allspice, and clove. On King's Day in 1946, the massive king cake brought to the center of the dining-room table was surrounded by small, gold-foil wrapped presents. My gift was a tiny golden medal of the Blessed Mother. That was when I was told that I would be representing Mary for my grandmother's St. Joseph Altar that upcoming spring. I could barely contain my elation and could not resist flaunting my exceptional status to each of my cousins.

Then comes Mardi Gras, Fat Tuesday, which always falls on the day before the beginning of Lent, Ash Wednesday. In South Louisiana, this time of year usually comes with cold and wet winter dreariness, but I recall coming back from parades to the soothing comfort of my grandmother's split pea soup, deliciously warm, velvety textured, rich with butter and olive oil, seasoned with basil, and topped with tiny pastina and a dollop of freshly grated Pecorino Romano. My Poppa Accardo was a member of the Mardi Gras Krewe of Virgilians, named for the Roman poet Virgil, and my mother and aunts were members of the Krewe of Venus. Most krewes traditionally served split pea soup to the float riders when they returned to their den, before they went to the balls.

In spite of the frenetic activity that takes place during Mardi Gras season, in 1946 it was during those hectic weeks that my grandmother began knitting a delicate pastel aqua-blue sweater for me to wear on St. Joseph's Feast Day. That year, well before Lundi Gras, the Monday before Mardi Gras, Mommie Accardo had assembled her crew for "Making the Altar." With St. Joseph's Day fast approaching, they had already prepared and packaged a luscious assortment of Sicilian biscotti. Throughout those endless hours of activity, tantalizing flavors of anise, almond, chocolate, cinnamon, clove, lemon, and orange filled her kitchen. The more delicate *cuccidati* were made in the weeks just prior to the March 19 feast day. I can still smell the aroma of the mounds of dried Greek figs my grandmother had blended with honey, cinnamon, and the pungent zest of Plaquemines Parish oranges. She finished spicing those figs with a scant toss of black pepper, which gave an Arabesque bite to the dried fruits' sweetness. To this day, *cuccidati* prepared in exactly that way remain a family favorite, and the cookies disappear as soon as they are baked.

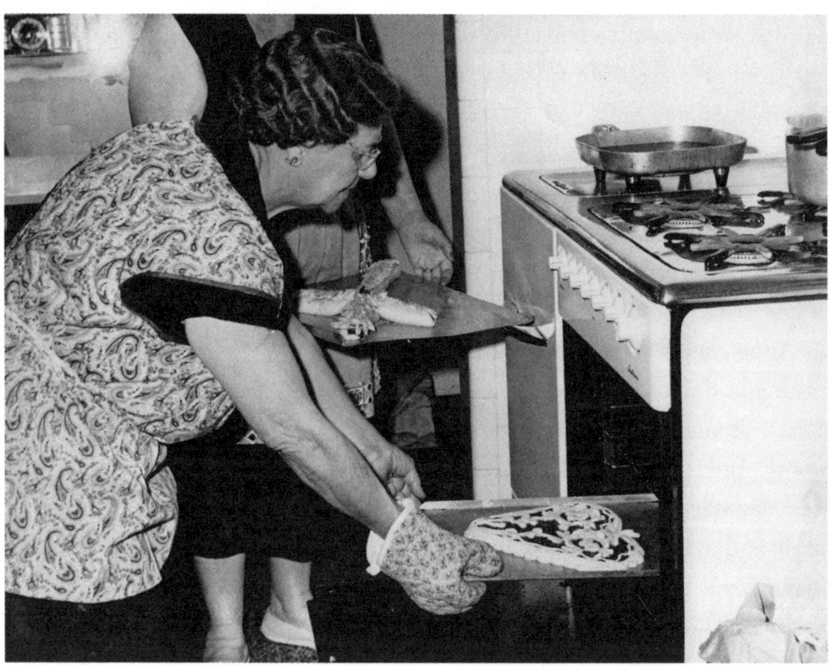

Nonna Accardo baking at home.

My anticipation for that special long-ago St. Joseph's Day was mixed with those delicious baking aromas coming from the kitchen, along with the soft, lyrical voices of my grandmother and her friends chanting in their Sicilian dialect, as they prayed the Novena of San Giuseppe, nine days of prayer before the feast day.

Finally, St. Joseph's Day arrived. I was dressed in a pleated white challis skirt topped by the soft aqua-blue sweater my grandmother had knitted. My hair was forced into big fat cascading curls that bounced as I walked slowly and solemnly in the *Tupa-Tupa* procession. The Holy Family that year was represented by my cousin Joseph, who portrayed Jesus, an older cousin who portrayed St. Joseph, and myself, portraying Mary. In the tradition of the procession, we knocked on three doors, those facing my grandmother's hallway, which led to the dining room. We were told at the first two, "There is no room for you here." When we knocked on the third door, as the door was swung open, I was so overwhelmed I barely heard the words, "Welcome. Come inside. The feast has been prepared for you!"

My grandmother's dining room had been totally and beautifully transformed, with three tiered tables laden with elaborate foods. As I walked inside, I remember being enveloped by the combined smells of the St. Joseph Altar—of flowers and candles, of fresh fruit and vegetables, of many flavored cookies, and the exquisite array of rich foods. It was an ambrosial aroma I can only describe as "food of the gods." To this day, whenever I experience that amazing smell, I am again filled with a complete sense of joy and excitement for participating in this sacred ancient tradition.

After the altar was blessed in a special ceremony, the priest who had presided over the blessing was seated with us, the Holy Family, at the head of the elegantly set table. With great ceremony, my grandmother and her sisters, my great-aunts, served each of us a small taste of foods selected from the altar. As I recall, my cousin Joseph wasn't too fond of such exotic foods as *pasta con le sarde* topped with *mudica* and batter-fried *carduni,* delicacies traditionally served for the St. Joseph's Day Feast. Since these blessed foods could not be wasted, I graciously offered to add his portion to mine.

I feel sure this single event was the awakening of my inherited Sicilian taste buds. I am particularly grateful for the legacy of this beautiful heritage, passed down and affectionately shared through countless generations. Recalling these many rituals bound in delicious memories, I know we who share in this sacred tradition have been truly blessed. For any child or adult who is honored to become a saint at a St. Joseph Altar, the rewards are boundless in the cherished memory of this special privilege.

5

Symbols of Hope

The lucky bean and the egg pastry known as *pupa cu l'ova* are two traditional, nonedible foods that grace St. Joseph Altars. The lucky bean is usually found on most St. Joseph Altars while not all altars will have *pupa cu l'ova*. Both are symbols of spring and hope, with histories going back many centuries.

Lucky Beans

The lucky bean is an essential element of the centuries-old St. Joseph Altar tradition. According to legend, during that lengthy drought in Sicily, when the crops were withering and the starving people were praying to St. Joseph for help, it was the humble fava bean, which grows well in poor soil, that became a lifesaver. Until this time of famine, fava beans had been used as cattle fodder. But hunger forced the population to eat them, and the nourishing beans became the symbol of their hope. After the drought ended and there were celebrations of thanksgiving in honor of St. Joseph's intercession, the tradition of the fava bean representing abundance was established.

When Sicilians arrived in Louisiana and transplanted their St. Joseph Altar tradition into the fertile soil of this state's many celebrations, they brought along their fava beans, which are believed by many to bring good fortune. The hardy bean is also a metaphor for the resilience of those Sicilian immigrants who cultivated the St. Joseph Altar traditions, for their descendants who nurtured those traditions, and for the multicultural groups whose hybrid of diverse ethnic artistry enriches the devotion.

Today, baskets or bowls of fava beans are always displayed on St. Joseph Altars as annual reminders of sharing in blessings from a bountiful harvest. Each visitor to a St. Joseph Altar is usually given a blessed lucky bean. Over the years, these dried beans have found their way into the pockets and purses of many and are kept as treasured mementos of the St. Joseph's Day celebration. May the lucky bean become for you a symbol of resilience and hope, fulfilling its promise of bountiful blessings.

Fava bean rosary. Photo by Anthony "Chopper" Leone.

ROASTED FAVA BEANS
(LUCKY BEANS)

Makes as many as you want

Before roasted fava beans can be distributed as lucky beans, they must be blessed at a St. Joseph Altar. Dried fava beans can be purchased by the pound, especially during the weeks prior to March 19, from Louisiana grocers such as Dorignac's Food Center and Nor-Joe's Import Company in Metairie (see Sources for Purchasing Specialty Supplies on page 15.) Once roasted, fava beans will last for years if kept dry. Keep in mind that roasted fava beans are not meant to be eaten. The following method is for preserving them as keepsakes.

1. Preheat oven to 350°F. Place dried fava beans in a shallow baking pan in a single layer. Bake until beans start to turn brown, shaking the pan occasionally and stirring and turning beans over. This should take 15–20 minutes.

2. Remove them from the pan to cool. Store at room temperature in a dry place. Will keep for many years.

Pupa cu l'Ova

Pupa cu l'ova (literally, "puppets with eggs"), also called *pupukolova* in some Sicilian dialects, are nonedible figurines made of pastry baked over a whole hard-boiled egg. Their origin goes back many centuries, to a time when a Papal edict forbade eating eggs during Lent. Unfortunately, no one explained this religious law to the chickens, who continued their springtime egg-laying routine with prolific proficiency.

Naturally, the frugal Sicilians did not want to waste the eggs laid during the six-week period of Lent. So, they became creative and fashioned pastry over dyed hard-boiled eggs and formed the dough into replicas of small chickens or baskets as toys for their children to play with. From the beginning, *pupa cu l'ova* were included in Easter baskets. Today, they are also usually displayed in pairs on St. Joseph Altars as springtime symbols of hope, renewal, and everlasting love.

As children of Sicilian heritage, my siblings, cousins, and I always found *pupa cu l'ova* tucked between sugared rabbits and chocolate eggs in our Easter baskets. It wasn't until I was a teenager that I learned how unusual this ancient Sicilian tradition was, and how very privileged we were to be the recipients of these gifts of love. I have since taught my relatives how to carve their own, which they now include in Easter baskets for their grandchildren.

PUPA CU L'OVA
(PUPPET WITH EGGS)

Makes 2

2½ cups all-purpose flour
2 tablespoons white vegetable shortening
½ cup sugar
¾–1 cup warm water (tepid, not boiling)
2 hard-boiled eggs, dyed the color of your choice
4 whole cloves

1. Preheat oven to 250°F. In a large bowl, combine flour and shortening and blend until the mixture resembles coarse cornmeal. Set aside.

2. In a separate smaller bowl, add sugar and gradually add ¾ cup warm water, stirring constantly until sugar is dissolved. Gradually add sugar water mixture to flour mixture and stir with a spoon until dough holds together enough so that you can form a ball. If dough seems too dry, gradually add remaining warm water. Cover and set aside 10 minutes.

Photo by Anthony "Chopper" Leone.

3. Separate the dough in half. On a hard surface, roll each dough half into a 10-inch square that's 1/4 inch thick. Cover one of the dough squares with plastic and set aside. Take the other dough sheet and from the side cut off a 1/2×10 inch strip. Roll the dough strip into a rope that's 1/2×8 inches and lay it on your work surface horizontally. Slide the left end of the rope below its center. Holding that end down, bring the right side of the rope down and over the left side to form an oval. Beyond where the rope crosses, leave an inch of dough on each end. (The exposed ends will become the feet.) Place the dough-rope oval onto parchment paper. Position an unpeeled dyed egg in the dough oval, with the egg's broad side lying on top of the crossed portion of the rope. The egg should fit snugly, with the larger side perching forward at a 45-degree angle.

4. From the remainder of the dough sheet, cut a 9-inch circle with a 1-inch triangle extending out of the top of the circle. (The triangle will become the head.) Bring the dough circle to the egg from behind, from the side opposite the feet. Lay the triangle over the highest point of the egg, being careful not to tear the triangle away from the rest of the dough. On the egg, pinch the dough triangle to stand up, thus forming the head.

5. Press enough of the attached dough circle over the egg to cover the rear 3/4 of the egg, which is behind the head. At the base of the egg, press together the rope base and the part of the dough circle that meets it. Be sure to seal the meeting point of the dough sheet and the rope tightly to form a secure base. Onto the parchment, fan out the remainder of the dough circle (which is most of it). This flat round of dough will become decorative feathering.

6. On the back of the egg just beneath the head, cut 6 evenly spaced vertical slits through the dough and down to the egg. Slice down to, but not into, the dough that fans out from the egg covering. Using a small paring knife, separate each space between the slits to reveal the dyed egg.

7. To simulate long feathers, cut decorative 1-inch slits along the entire edge of the circle of dough that fans out. To simulate small feathers, use small scissors to prick the inside portion of the dough fan. At the front of the head, make a single scissors-cut into the dough to form the mouth. For eyes, press one whole clove on each side of the head. Using scissors, cut two slits into the head to form a crown. To make claws, use a small knife to cut two slits each

into the 1-inch dough projections at the base of the *pupa cu l'ova*. Repeat the process with the second square of dough.

8. Bake the *pupa cu l'ova* until the dough is bone dry, but not browned, approximately one hour. Completely cooled *pupa cu l'ova* can be kept at room temperature for several weeks as decorative figurines only, not meant to be eaten!

6

Savory Dishes of San Giuseppe's Feast

Because the Feast of St. Joseph is celebrated during the solemn season of Lent, a period with a history of rules for abstaining from eating meat, foods prepared for the St. Joseph's Feast are meatless. Savory dishes center on delectable preparations of breads, fish, pasta, and a wondrous assortment of vegetables at their springtime prime.

Antipasti and Salads

CLASSIC RISOTTO

Makes 6 cups

8 tablespoons (1 stick) unsalted butter
1 medium onion, finely chopped
2 cups raw Arborio rice
4 cups chicken stock, warmed, divided
1 pinch saffron
½ cup white wine, warmed
6 tablespoons grated Parmesan cheese
1 teaspoon black pepper
Dash of freshly grated nutmeg

1. In a large skillet set over medium-high heat, melt the butter and add chopped onion. Simmer until onion is soft and translucent, 3 minutes. Reduce heat to medium. Using a wooden spoon, stir in the rice and thoroughly coat each grain with the butter.

2. Add saffron into one cup of stock and stir to fully incorporate. Set aside. Reduce heat under the skillet to a simmer. Ladle remaining 3 cups stock into rice, one cupful at a time, stirring with each addition until stock is absorbed. Add the saffron-infused stock and continue stirring until all liquid has been absorbed.

3. Pour in the wine and simmer until it is fully absorbed by the rice. Remove from heat and mix in the Parmesan cheese. Season with pepper and nutmeg. Total cooking time should be 18 to 20 minutes. By then, the rice should be tender and creamy but should still have some bite to it. Serve immediately. Leftover risotto can be used to make *arancini,* Sicilian fried rice balls.

ARANCINI
(FRIED RICE BALLS)

Makes twenty 2-inch balls

Arancini is the Sicilian word for oranges, and these savory appetizers are called *arancini* because they resemble the shape and golden color of an orange. In Palermo, these fried rice balls are a popular street food. They are also often served on an antipasto platter or as a first-course appetizer.

NOTE: *The small end of a melon-baller is the perfect size for cutting these balls.*

2 cups cooked and thoroughly chilled risotto (recipe page 37)
½ cup fresh, finely chopped flat-leafed Italian parsley
4 tablespoons thinly sliced fresh basil
¼ teaspoon freshly grated nutmeg
Ground black pepper to taste
3 large eggs, divided
½ cup fresh mozzarella, cut into 20 small rounds or ½-inch cubes
1 cup all-purpose flour
2 cups plain bread crumbs
2 quarts vegetable oil for deep frying
FOR SERVING: Basic Sicilian-Style Tomato Gravy (recipe page 68)

1. In a large bowl, combine chilled risotto with parsley, basil, nutmeg, and black pepper.

2. Lightly whisk 2 eggs and mix gently into the cold risotto mixture. Wet or oil your hands and spread 1 tablespoon of the risotto mixture into the palm of one hand. Press a piece of mozzarella into the center of the mixture and top it with another tablespoon of risotto. Finish by shaping into a 2-inch ball, being careful to completely surround the cheese with risotto.

3. Set up three shallow bowls. Place flour in one bowl, the remaining egg (slightly beaten) in another, and the bread crumbs in the other. Roll each rice ball first in flour, then gently in the beaten egg. Transfer it to the bowl to coat with bread crumbs and continue until each ball is thoroughly coated. Chill until firm, several hours, or refrigerate overnight. At this point, you can refrigerate your *arancini* up to two days or freeze them up to 2 weeks.

4. When ready to cook, use medium-high heat to preheat the oil to 350°F. Gently drop each ball into hot oil. (Frozen *arancini* do not have to be defrosted.) Fry, turning occasionally until golden on all sides, about 3 minutes. (For frozen *arancini,* test for doneness by inserting a knife into the center. If fully cooked, the tip of the knife should be warm, not cold.)

5. Drain on paper towels and serve immediately with tomato gravy on the side, if desired. To keep warm, place fried *arancini* in a 250°F oven up to 30 minutes.

CAPONATINA
(EGGPLANT RELISH)

Makes 3 quarts or twelve 8-ounce jars

This Sicilian-style sweet and tart eggplant relish was a specialty of my paternal grandmother, Virginia Maturana Scalise. Packaged into decorative jars, *caponatina* is always a welcome hostess gift.

2 large eggplants, unpeeled, rinsed, and dried
1 cup extra virgin olive oil, divided
Salt and black pepper
1 stalk celery, cut into ½-inch slices, leafy tops reserved
1 large onion, coarsely chopped
1 can (6 ounces) tomato paste
1½–2 cups sugar, divided
1 teaspoon ground cinnamon
1 cup white wine vinegar
1 large can (28 ounces) whole tomatoes, drained, liquid reserved
½ cup sliced fresh basil
2 tablespoons dried oregano
2 cups chopped olives with pimentos, rinsed and drained
1 cup pine nuts, toasted
½ cup pickled caper berries, rinsed and drained
4–5 tablespoons balsamic vinegar
FOR SERVING: lettuce leaves or toasted Italian bread slices

1. Preheat oven to 350°F. Cut eggplants into 1-inch cubes. Place eggplant cubes in a shallow baking pan, drizzle with ½ cup olive oil, and lightly salt and pepper to taste. Toss evenly to distribute. Roast until slightly browned, about 20 minutes. Turn the pieces over and roast until slightly browned on all sides, about 10 more minutes. Set aside.

2. In a large, heavy saucepan over medium heat, warm the remaining ½ cup of olive oil. Sauté celery just until translucent, about 5 minutes. Remove celery and set aside, leaving oil in the saucepan. Add onion to the saucepan and cook until translucent, about 7 minutes.

3. Reduce heat to low, add tomato paste, and bring to a simmer. Stir in 1 cup sugar and the cinnamon and stir constantly while the mixture simmers. Cook until mixture turns from bright red to a dark brick red color, about 5 minutes. Gradually blend in white wine vinegar.

Photo by Anthony "Chopper" Leone.

4. Cut canned tomatoes into medium-sized pieces. Gently stir tomatoes into the simmering mixture in the saucepan. Gradually add reserved tomato liquid. Season lightly with salt and pepper.

5. Stirring gently with a wooden spoon, carefully blend in the cooked eggplant and celery. Cook on medium heat, covered, for 15 minutes. Remove from heat. Chop the celery leaves. Add celery leaves, basil, and oregano to the pot. Fold in olives. Add pine nuts, capers, and 4 tablespoons balsamic vinegar. Taste and correct seasonings. Add more sugar if too tart, or the remaining tablespoon balsamic vinegar if too sweet.

6. Spoon hot caponatina into sterilized jars and seal according to manufacturer's directions. Allow sealed jars to cool completely to room temperature, then refrigerate up to two months. If not sealing into jars, allow mixture to cool to room temperature. Before serving, refrigerate at least overnight. *Caponatina* that is not canned and sealed will keep covered and refrigerated up to 2 weeks. Serve chilled as an antipasto with a side of toasted Italian bread slices, or on lettuce leaves as a salad.

CANNELLINI BEAN SALAD

Makes 6–8 servings

Water and ice cubes
½ cup thinly sliced red onion
2 (15.5-ounce) cans cannellini beans, rinsed and thoroughly drained
½ cup grape tomatoes, sliced in half lengthwise
2 tablespoons sliced, fresh basil
2 tablespoons minced, fresh flat-leafed parsley
½ cup extra virgin olive oil
¼ cup white balsamic vinegar
Salt and black pepper to taste
½ cup Gorgonzola cheese, crumbled

1. Chill a medium bowl in the refrigerator. Halfway fill a separate medium bowl with water and ice cubes and add sliced onion rings. Cover bowl and refrigerate. In the empty chilled bowl, add beans, tomatoes, basil and parsley.

2. In a jar or small bowl, whisk together olive oil, vinegar, salt, and pepper. Drizzle over beans and lightly toss. Refrigerate several hours or overnight.

3. Just before serving, drain the onions and toss them into the salad. Add Gorgonzola cheese and toss lightly. Serve immediately on chilled plates.

FAVA BEAN SALAD

Makes 4–6 servings

Water and ice cubes
1 small red onion, sliced into thin rounds
½ tablespoon salt
3 pounds (3¾ cups) fresh fava beans, shelled (3 pounds of unshelled fava beans will yield approximately 3 cups of beans)
½ cup extra virgin olive oil
¼ cup white balsamic vinegar
½ teaspoon Mediterranean Sea salt
¼ teaspoon freshly ground black pepper
1 cup fresh anise, cleaned, coarsely chopped, leafy fronds reserved, or 1 cup fresh fennel, cleaned, thinly sliced, leafy fronds reserved
FOR SERVING: 4 cups lettuce leaves, rinsed and chilled

1. Halfway fill a medium bowl with water and ice cubes and add sliced onion rounds. Cover bowl and refrigerate. Prepare another bowl of ice water for the beans.

2. Bring a saucepan of water to a boil and add the salt. Return to a full boil and add fava beans. Cook 1 minute. With a slotted spoon or spatula, remove beans into the prepared bowl of iced water. Set aside to cool. When beans are cool, drain them, peel off and discard outer skins, and set them aside.

3. Chill a medium serving bowl. Meanwhile, make a vinaigrette by whisking together in a jar or small bowl the olive oil, vinegar, salt, and pepper. In the chilled bowl, lightly mix fava beans and anise. Toss with vinaigrette. Thoroughly drain onion rings and lightly toss into salad. Add 2 tablespoons leafy anise fronds. At this point the salad can be refrigerated up to several hours.

4. When ready to serve, arrange lettuce leaves on chilled plates. Spoon fava bean salad into the center of lettuce and toss remaining anise fronds onto each plate. Serve immediately.

GREEN BEAN SALAD

Makes 4–6 servings

Water for boiling
1 tablespoon salt
1 pound small new potatoes, skins scrubbed and cut into quarters
Ice cubes and water
1 pound fresh green beans, strings and ends removed, cut into thirds or halves
½ cup extra virgin olive oil
¼ cup white balsamic vinegar
½ teaspoon Mediterranean Sea salt
¼ teaspoon freshly ground black pepper
½ cup freshly grated Parmesan cheese
4 tablespoons sliced fresh basil leaves

1. Bring a saucepan of water to boil and add the salt. Return to a full boil and add potato quarters. Boil until fork-tender, about 10 minutes. Chill a serving bowl, and put ice cubes and water halfway up in a medium-sized mixing bowl. Leaving the water in the pan, use a slotted spoon or spatula to remove the potatoes and place them into the bowl of iced water. Set the potatoes aside to cool.

2. Drain cooled potatoes and transfer into the chilled bowl. Return salted water to full boil. Add green beans and cook just until fork-tender, about 3–5 minutes. Remove green beans into a fresh bowl of iced water. Drain cooled green beans and add to the bowl with chilled potatoes.

3. Make a vinaigrette in a jar or small bowl by whisking together olive oil, vinegar, salt, and pepper. Lightly toss salad with vinaigrette, Parmesan cheese, and basil. Serve immediately on chilled plates or chill several hours or overnight.

SICILIAN-STYLE OLIVE SALAD

Makes 1 quart

½ cup extra virgin olive oil
¼ cup balsamic vinegar
2 teaspoons freshly ground black pepper
2 cups pitted green olives with pimentos, rinsed and thoroughly drained
1 cup coarsely chopped celery
1 cup shredded carrots
½ cup thinly sliced fresh basil
2 tablespoons minced fresh flat-leafed Italian parsley
⅓ cup finely chopped fresh lemon, including rind and pulp
1 tablespoon crushed fresh oregano
½ cup freshly grated Parmesan cheese

1. Chill a medium mixing bowl. Meanwhile, make a vinaigrette in a small bowl or jar by combining oil, vinegar, and pepper. Set aside.

2. Into the chilled bowl, toss together olives, celery, carrots, basil, and parsley. Add the lemon and oregano and toss with vinaigrette. Add Parmesan cheese and lightly toss to thoroughly mix. Keeps in the refrigerator in tightly closed jars up to a week.

SICILIAN-STYLE POTATO SALAD

Makes 8 servings

Water
Table salt
4 cups new potatoes, peeled and sliced into ½-inch rounds
Ice cubes
1 yellow onion, medium chopped
½ cup, plus 2 tablespoons extra virgin olive oil
¼ cup white balsamic vinegar
2 teaspoons Mediterranean Sea salt
Ground black pepper to taste
2 (14-ounce) cans quartered artichoke hearts, rinsed, drained, and chilled
2 tablespoons sliced fresh basil
2 tablespoons minced fresh flat-leafed Italian parsley
1 tablespoon crushed fresh oregano
1 (2-ounce) jar pickled capers, rinsed, drained, and chilled
½ cup freshly grated Parmesan cheese
FOR SERVING: 4 cups lettuce leaves, rinsed, drained, and chilled

1. Bring a large pot of salted water to a boil and add potatoes. Reduce heat to medium and cook just until fork tender, about 10 minutes. Fill a large bowl halfway with ice cubes and water. Remove potatoes with a slotted spoon into the ice water bath.

2. In a microwave-safe bowl, toss together onion with 2 tablespoons olive oil. Cook in the microwave on high power just until soft, about 1 minute. Set aside and cool to room temperature.

3. Chill a large bowl. Meanwhile, make a vinaigrette in a jar or small bowl by mixing together ½ cup olive oil, balsamic vinegar, sea salt, and pepper. Set aside.

4. When potatoes are thoroughly chilled, drain and put them in the chilled bowl. Add the cooled onions, artichoke hearts, basil, parsley, and oregano. Lightly toss with vinaigrette. Chill until ready to serve or overnight.

5. Just before serving, toss the potato salad lightly with thoroughly drained capers. Top with a sprinkling of grated Parmesan cheese. Serve chilled on a bed of lettuce leaves.

BACCALÀ
(FRIED SALT COD)

Makes 6 servings (Begin a day ahead.)

2 pounds salted codfish
Water
2 cups milk
2 large eggs
1 cup all-purpose flour
¼ teaspoon ground black pepper
2 cups vegetable oil
FOR SERVING: 2 lemons, cut into wedges

1. Cover codfish with cold water and soak 12–18 hours in the refrigerator. During the soaking period, drain and add fresh water at least three times. Rinse fish under running water. Cut each fillet into 2-inch pieces. Place fish pieces in a deep glass dish, cover with milk, and refrigerate overnight.

2. When ready to cook, in a shallow bowl, lightly beat eggs. Add flour and stir to form a paste. Stir in black pepper.

3. In a deep skillet, heat oil to 375°F. Oil is ready when a dollop of egg-flour paste dropped in rises to the top. Drain fish and discard milk. Roll fish pieces in egg and flour paste, thoroughly coating each piece. A few at a time, drop fish into heated oil, carefully avoiding crowding. Cook until golden on both sides and drain on paper towels. Fried fish can be kept warm up to 15 minutes in a 200°F oven. To serve, transfer fish to a warmed plate and surround with lemon wedges.

PESCE AL FORNO, VINO ROSSO (STUFFED REDFISH BAKED IN TOMATO-WINE SAUCE)

Makes 8–10 servings

The centerpiece on most St. Joseph Altars, this baked, stuffed redfish is usually placed on the altar for the Blessing. After the Blessing, it's refrigerated and then rewarmed before serving.

The Tomato-Wine Sauce can be prepared ahead and frozen. The Fish Stock and Redfish Dressing can also be frozen ahead of time, but to do so you'll have to prepare them with the center bone from a fish you are not planning to display at the Blessing or serve at the altar.

Fish Preparation

A 4- or 5-pound whole redfish or red snapper, with head and tail on

1. Remove fish's eyes, scales, gills, and entrails. To make a pocket for stuffing, turn fish onto its side and slice the belly open all the way from head to tail and deep into the center of the flesh.

2. Cut out the center bone, the long bone inside the upper part of the cavity that runs the length of the fish. Rinse the center bone, leaving on any attached meat, and discard loose bones. Refrigerate the center bone and any meat that has fallen off for Fish Stock. Rinse the fish well, including the pocket, and carefully remove any loose bones. Pat dry, cover, and refrigerate until ready to cook.

Fish Stock

Makes about 2 quarts

This stock is meant for use in the Redfish Dressing and in the Tomato-Wine Sauce, but it's also good in any seafood-based dish.

4 quarts water
3–4 teaspoons salt
1 small onion, cut into quarters
2 ribs celery, cut in half
2 bay leaves
2 tablespoons Zatarain's Crab Boil mix, removed from boiling bag
Center bone of fish, including attached meat and any extra bits of meat
Shrimp shells and heads from shrimp used for Redfish Dressing (recipe below), eyes and tentacles removed
½ lemon, juice and peel

1. Bring water to a full boil. Add 3 teaspoons salt, onion, celery, bay leaves, and crab boil. Return to full boil. Add fish bone, shrimp shells and heads, and lemon. Continue cooking on medium heat 15 minutes, skimming off and discarding foam as it rises to the top.

2. Remove fish bone. Remove meat from the bone, and spoon any meat out of the stock. Set the meat bits aside for dressing, and discard the bone. Taste the stock, and if needed add up to 1 teaspoon salt. Simmer stock 15 minutes. Strain stock and set aside. When prepared with a center bone from another fish, Fish Stock can be made ahead and frozen up to 1 week.

Redfish Dressing (for stuffing the fish)

2 cups torn French bread, toasted
1 cup Fish Stock (from recipe above)
½ cup olive oil
1 medium yellow onion, chopped
1 cup chopped celery
1 cup medium shrimp, cleaned and deveined
1 teaspoon salt
½ teaspoon black pepper
2 pinches cayenne pepper
1 cup cooked fish, removed from boiled center bone
1 (28-ounce) can Italian plum tomatoes, drained, liquid reserved, and tomatoes chopped, divided
1 cup fresh crabmeat, shells removed
½ cup plain bread crumbs
1 bay leaf
4 tablespoons chopped fresh flat-leafed Italian parsley
4 tablespoons sliced fresh basil
2 tablespoons crushed fresh oregano

1. Soak toasted bread in fish stock until well saturated. Squeeze bread dry and set aside. Warm olive oil in a heavy skillet set over medium heat. Sauté onion just until translucent, about 6 minutes. Add celery and cook 3 minutes. Turn heat to high and add shrimp. Cook until they turn pink, about 3 minutes.

2. Add the salt, pepper, and cayenne. Stir in the cooked fish. Gradually stir in the squeezed bread and cook until bread slightly sticks to the bottom of the pan. Scrape up the browned bits and fold into the mixture. Thoroughly stir in 1 cup chopped tomatoes. (Reserve remaining tomatoes and liquid for the Tomato-Wine Sauce.) Stir in crabmeat, bread crumbs, bay leaf, parsley, basil, and oregano. When prepared with the center bone from a fish other than the one you're serving at the Blessing of the Altar, Redfish Dressing can be made ahead and frozen up to 1 week.

Tomato-Wine Sauce

Makes about a quart

Use this savory sauce for basting the fish and for serving.

½ cup olive oil
1 medium onion, minced
1 cup finely chopped celery
Remaining chopped tomatoes and tomato liquid from Redfish Dressing recipe
1 (15-ounce) can tomato sauce
Salt and ground black pepper to taste
2 cups fish stock (recipe page 49)
1 cup Pinot Grigio or other dry white wine
4 tablespoons chopped fresh flat-leafed Italian parsley
4 tablespoons sliced fresh basil
2 tablespoons crushed fresh oregano

1. Add the olive oil to a large saucepan set over high heat. When oil is hot, cook the onion until caramelized, about 3 minutes. Add celery and cook until translucent, about 2 minutes. Reduce heat. Add chopped tomatoes, tomato liquid, and tomato sauce and simmer 5 minutes.

2. Season with salt and black pepper. Return to high heat. Add stock and wine and boil vigorously until liquid reduces by half, about 3 minutes. Remove from heat and stir in parsley, basil, and oregano. Set aside. Tomato-wine sauce can be made ahead and frozen up to 1 week.

Baking the Fish

Cleaned fish, prepared for stuffing
1 cup olive oil, divided
1 teaspoon Mediterranean Sea salt
½ teaspoon freshly cracked black pepper
Redfish Dressing (recipe page 50, at room temperature)
6 (9¾-inch) wood skewers
1 large yellow onion, cut into thick rounds
1 cup Pinot Grigio or other dry white wine
Tomato-Wine Sauce (recipe above)

1. Heat oven to 375°F. Brush fish with ¾ cup olive oil, thoroughly coating outside and inside pocket. Sprinkle all over with salt and black pepper.

2. Place Redfish Dressing in a heavy skillet set over medium heat and stir until completely warmed through, 8–10 minutes. Stuff warm Redfish Dressing into fish's pocket and secure in place with wood skewers.

3. Coat the bottom of a large, shallow baking pan with remaining ¼ cup olive oil. Arrange onion rounds evenly on the bottom of the pan. Place the whole, stuffed fish onto the onion rings. Cover tail and head with foil. Add wine to bottom of pan. Place in preheated oven and bake 30 minutes. Remove from oven.

4. Remove foil from head and tail of fish. Pour 2 cups Tomato-Wine Sauce around the fish. Carefully spoon ½ cup sauce over the fish. Return to oven and bake 15 minutes. Remove from oven and allow fish to stand 10 minutes before going to the final step.

Garnish and Serve

3 lemons, sliced into rounds, seeds removed
Fresh curly parsley, stems removed, rinsed and dried on paper towels
½ cup sliced stuffed olives with pimentos, drained well
½ cup pickled caper berries, rinsed and drained
A toothpick
1 whole stuffed olive
Remainder of Tomato-Wine Sauce

1. Carefully place baked fish onto a heated serving platter or an attractive large wooden board. Reserve one lemon slice and arrange the remainder around the outside of fish. Tuck parsley between the lemon slices. Scatter sliced olives and caper berries over fish. Use a toothpick to secure the reserved lemon slice and the whole stuffed olive into the fish's eye socket.

2. To serve, cut the fish into 2-inch slices, each with an upper and lower layer of fish, with dressing in-between. Top individual servings with warmed Tomato-Wine Sauce.

Vegetables

It is said that, during the days of preparations before St. Joseph's Day, if you happen into any kitchen in the midst of cooking specialty vegetables for the altar, "you are likely to be stuffed!" The long-standing tradition of stuffing or topping vegetables with bread crumbs goes back to the Sicilian custom of using leftover bread in a variety of creative ways.

CARCIOFI FRITTI
(FRIED FRESH ARTICHOKE HEARTS)

Makes 24 pieces

The flowering head of a sticky thistle, the artichoke was grown as far back as the fifth century BC in Sicily. However, it was the French who originally brought the artichoke to New Orleans, where the vegetable was sold in the public market as early as the 1740s. Fried artichoke hearts were a Sunday dinner specialty of my grandmother Scalise.

4 large fresh artichokes
3 lemons, 1 cut in half and 2 cut into wedges
2 large eggs
1 cup all-purpose flour
1 teaspoon salt
¼ teaspoon ground black pepper
½ cup olive oil

1. With a serrated knife, cut off 2 inches from tops of artichokes. Leaving stems intact, cut off and discard outer leaves, peeling into the tender light-colored heart of the artichoke. Cut each artichoke in half lengthwise, cutting through the stem. Cut each artichoke half into thirds lengthwise. You should have 24 pieces.

2. Remove tough thistles and fuzzy chokes from inside each artichoke piece. Rinse trimmed artichoke pieces under running water to thoroughly clean off any clinging fuzzy choke. Drain well on paper towels. Use half-cut lemons to rub lemon juice all over each artichoke piece. Set them aside.

3. In a shallow bowl, lightly beat eggs. Add flour and stir to form a paste. Stir in salt and black pepper. Heat olive oil in a deep skillet to 350°F. Oil is ready when a dollop of egg-flour paste dropped in rises to the top. Dredge artichoke pieces in paste and carefully drop them into hot oil. Fry until golden on both sides, turning once. Drain on paper towels.

4. Serve on a warmed platter and garnish with lemon wedges. Fried artichoke hearts can be kept warm up to 15 minutes in a 200°F oven.

STUFFED ARTICHOKES

Makes 6 whole stuffed artichokes

Whole artichokes filled with seasoned bread crumbs, cheese, olive oil, and herbs are as much a part of local cuisine as are red gravy and cannoli. And it was Sicilian immigrants who made this particular recipe popular in New Orleans.

- 6 large fresh artichokes
- 4 cups plain or seasoned bread crumbs
- 3 cups freshly grated Parmesan cheese
- 2 teaspoons salt
- 1 teaspoon ground black pepper
- 6 tablespoons chopped fresh flat-leafed parsley
- 6 tablespoons chopped fresh basil
- 3 tablespoons crushed fresh oregano
- 1 cup olive oil, divided
- 1 cup caciocavallo cheese, cut into ½-inch wedges
- 2 cups warmed (not boiling) water, divided
- 1 lemon, sliced into 6 rounds

1. Trim away and discard stems from artichokes. Slice bottoms of artichokes evenly so they can stand upright. Remove and discard any discolored outer leaves. With kitchen shears, cut the pointed tips off each leaf. Use a large serrated knife or scissors to cut 1 inch off the tops of the artichokes. Under running water, open up the leaves. Scoop out and discard the choke from the center of the artichokes and rinse the insides thoroughly. Stand artichokes upside down on a wire rack to drain off excess liquid.

2. In a large bowl, mix together bread crumbs, Parmesan cheese, salt, and pepper. Add parsley, basil, and oregano. Mix in ½ cup of olive oil. Evenly distribute and tuck caciocavallo cheese wedges into leaves of each artichoke. Hold one artichoke over the bowl of the bread-crumb and cheese mixture and fill each leaf, as well as the center, with the mixture. Fill all the artichokes the same way, packing with the bread-crumb mixture as tightly as possible.

3. Place the stuffed artichokes upright in a heavy-bottomed pot, preferably standing them on a wire rack that will hold them above the pot's bottom. Puncture the tops of the stuffed artichokes with a wooden skewer. Drizzle remaining ½ cup olive oil over the artichoke tops, allowing olive oil to seep into the stuffing.

4. Add 1 cup warmed water into pot around the artichokes. Cover pot tightly and cook on medium heat at least 1 hour. Add another ½ cup warm water around artichokes, reduce heat to a simmer, and continue to cook another 45 minutes. Test for doneness by removing one leaf, which will have a glossy look when fully cooked and should come off easily. If artichokes are not fully cooked, add another ½ cup of water and continue to cook. Depending on the size of artichokes, cooking time can vary from one to two hours.

5. When artichokes are fully cooked, carefully remove them to a large serving platter. Place a lemon slice on top of each artichoke and serve immediately. Thoroughly cooled artichokes can be refrigerated for several days. If securely wrapped, they can be frozen for several weeks.

FRIED CABBAGE

Makes 6–8 servings

2 quarts water
1 small head green cabbage
Toothpicks
1 tablespoon plus 1 teaspoon salt
3 cups plain or seasoned bread crumbs
1 cup freshly grated Parmesan cheese
3 tablespoons minced, fresh flat-leafed Italian parsley
2 tablespoons thinly sliced fresh basil
1 tablespoon crushed fresh oregano
1 teaspoon ground black pepper
2 large eggs, slightly beaten
2 cups vegetable oil, divided
FOR SERVING: 1 lemon, sliced lengthwise into 8 wedges

1. Bring water to a boil in a large pot. Meanwhile, cut the head of cabbage into 8 to 10 wedges. Skewer each wedge with a toothpick. Add 1 tablespoon salt to the boiling water and return to a full boil. Add cabbage wedges to boiling water and cook just until tender, about 3 minutes. Remove with a slotted spoon to drain. Set aside to cool.

2. In a shallow pan, mix together bread crumbs, cheese, parsley, basil, oregano, black pepper, and 1 teaspoon salt. Set aside. Add eggs to a separate shallow bowl and whisk to a slight froth. Working with one cabbage wedge at a time, dip into egg, then coat with bread-crumb mixture. Set wedges aside until they are all coated. Coated cabbage wedges can be refrigerated several hours before frying.

3. When ready to cook, heat 1 cup oil in a shallow skillet set over medium heat until it's hot, about 350°F. Add several pieces of the coated cabbage, being careful to avoid overcrowding. Fry to a light golden brown, turning to cook on all sides. Drain cooked wedges on paper towels, and then transfer them to a warmed plate. Before starting the second batch, remove any browned bits of bread crumbs from skillet and heat the remaining cup of oil to temperature.

4. After all the cabbage is fried and drained, remove the toothpicks. Fried cabbage can be kept warm up to 15 minutes in 200°F oven. Serve garnished with lemon wedges.

FRIED CARDUNI
(CARDOONS)

Makes 24–36 pieces

Carduni are large stalk-like vegetables with deep-green leaves and a flavor resembling artichokes. This springtime specialty is traditionally served fried for the St. Joseph Altar Feast.

1 bunch cardoons (3 to 4 large stalks)
4 quarts water
1 tablespoon plus 1 teaspoon salt
2 lemons, one quartered and one cut into wedges
2 large eggs
1 cup all-purpose flour
¼ teaspoon ground black pepper
Vegetable oil for frying

1. Separate the stalks of *carduni.* Cut away and discard outside leaves and remove strings as you would for celery. Rinse and thoroughly drain. Cut each stalk of cleaned *carduni* into approximately 3-inch-long pieces.

2. Bring water to a boil in a large pot. Add one tablespoon salt and lemon quarters and return to a full boil. Add *carduni* and boil until fork-tender, about 20 minutes. Drain and set aside to cool. Boiled carduni can be refrigerated up to three days before frying.

3. When ready to fry, in a shallow bowl, lightly beat eggs. Add flour and stir to form a paste. Season with remaining teaspoon of salt and black pepper.

4. In a deep skillet, heat oil to 375°F. Oil is ready to fry when a dollop of egg-flour paste dropped in rises to the top. Dip *carduni* pieces in the egg paste and drop into hot oil, being careful to avoid overcrowding. Fry until golden on both sides, turning once. Drain on paper towels. *Carduni* can be kept warm up to 15 minutes in a 200°F oven. Serve warm, surrounded by lemon wedges.

FRIED CAULIFLOWER

Makes 6–8 servings

1 medium head cauliflower
2 quarts water
2 tablespoons, plus 1 teaspoon salt
Large bowl with 2 quarts iced water
2 cups plain or seasoned bread crumbs
1 cup freshly grated Parmesan cheese
2 tablespoons sliced fresh basil
3 tablespoons minced fresh flat-leafed Italian parsley
1 tablespoon crushed fresh oregano
1 teaspoon ground black pepper
2 large eggs, slightly beaten
2 cups vegetable oil, divided

1. Separate cauliflower into individual florets. Rinse and remove any brown spots. In a large pot, bring water to boil. Add 1 tablespoon salt and return to a full boil. Add cauliflower florets to boiling water and cook 2 minutes. With a slotted spoon, remove florets to iced water. When florets are cool, remove and set aside to thoroughly drain.

2. In a shallow pan, mix together bread crumbs, cheese, basil, parsley, oregano, 1 teaspoon salt, and black pepper. Set aside. Add eggs to a separate shallow bowl and whisk to a slight froth. Working with one cauliflower floret at a time, dip into egg, then coat with bread-crumb mixture. Set aside until all florets are coated. Coated cauliflower florets can be refrigerated several hours until ready to fry.

3. In a shallow skillet set over medium heat, heat 1 cup oil until it's hot, about 350°F. Add several coated florets at a time, being careful to avoid overcrowding. Fry to a light golden brown on all sides. Drain cooked cauliflower on paper towels and then transfer to a warmed plate. Before cooking second batch, remove any browned bread-crumb bits from skillet and heat the remaining cup of oil. Cook remaining cauliflower florets. Fried cauliflower can be kept warm up to 15 minutes in a 200°F oven. Serve them warm.

CUCUZZA
(SICILIAN-STYLE STEWED SQUASH)

Makes one 2-quart casserole or 8 individual ramekins

Cucuzza is a hard, light-green gourd type of squash with creamy white flesh. It is straight or slightly curved and can reach a length of thirty-six inches.

½ cup olive oil
1 large yellow onion, chopped
½ green bell pepper, chopped
4 cups *cucuzza* squash, cut into 2-inch cubes (For smaller, young *cucuzza,* leave skin on. For large, older *cucuzza,* peel and discard tough outer skin. Remove and discard large seeds.)
2 cups fresh tomatoes (preferably Creole), blanched, skins removed, and quartered
Salt and black pepper to taste
2 cups freshly grated Parmesan cheese, divided
4 tablespoons minced fresh, flat-leafed Italian parsley
4 tablespoons sliced fresh basil
4 tablespoons butter, plus more for buttering baking dish
1 cup plain or seasoned bread crumbs
1 teaspoon paprika

Photo by Anthony "Chopper" Leone.

1. Preheat oven to 350°F. Set a heavy skillet over medium heat and warm the olive oil. Add onion and cook until translucent, about 6 minutes. Add bell pepper and continue cooking until limp, about 3 more minutes. Add *cucuzza* and stir and cook until translucent, about 8 minutes.

2. Increase heat to high. Add tomatoes and cook until liquid evaporates. As mixture begins to stick, stir and scrape up from the bottom. Season lightly with salt and pepper. Remove from heat, then stir in 1 cup Parmesan cheese, parsley, and basil. Taste and correct seasonings.

3. Butter the insides of a 2-quart baking casserole or 8 individual ramekins, and spoon in cooked *cucuzza*. Mix together bread crumbs, remaining cup of Parmesan cheese, and paprika. Sprinkle bread-crumb mixture over *cucuzza*. Dot with butter. Bake until warmed through and top is browned, about 20 minutes. Serve immediately. Cooked *cucuzza,* ether baked or unbaked, freezes well. If frozen before baking, defrost to room temperature and bake as directed.

FRIED EGGPLANT

Makes 6 servings

1 large eggplant
2 cups plain or seasoned bread crumbs
1 cup freshly grated Parmesan cheese
4 tablespoons minced fresh flat-leafed Italian parsley
2 tablespoons thinly sliced fresh basil
1 tablespoon crushed fresh oregano
1 teaspoon ground black pepper
2 large eggs, slightly beaten
2 cups vegetable oil, divided
FOR SERVING: ½ cup parsley sprigs, 1 cup shaved Parmesan cheese, and 2 cups Basic Sicilian-Style Tomato Gravy (recipe page 68)

1. Remove stem end from eggplant. Leaving skin on, cut eggplant lengthwise into ½-inch-thick slices. Set the slabs of eggplant aside.

2. In a shallow bowl, mix together bread crumbs, Parmesan cheese, parsley, basil, oregano, and black pepper. Set aside. Add eggs to a separate shallow bowl and whisk to a slight froth. Working with one eggplant slice at a time,

dip into egg, then coat with bread-crumb mixture. Set aside until all eggplant slices are coated.

3. Heat 1 cup vegetable oil in a shallow skillet set over medium heat. When oil is hot, approximately, 350°F, add several coated eggplant slices at a time and cook both sides until golden brown, 2–3 minutes per side. Remove cooked eggplant to a warmed plate. Before cooking remaining eggplant, remove any browned bits of bread crumbs from skillet. Heat remaining cup of oil and cook remaining eggplant slices until golden brown on both sides. Garnish with parsley sprigs, top with shaved Parmesan, and serve immediately with tomato gravy on the side. Fried Eggplant can be kept warm up to 15 minutes in a 200°F oven.

EGGPLANT PARMESAN

Makes 6 servings

1½ cups Basic Sicilian-Style Tomato Gravy, warmed (recipe page 68)
Fried Eggplant (recipe above)
4 ounces (6 slices) Provolone cheese

Preheat oven to 350°F. In the bottom of a 2-quart casserole dish, ladle ½ cup tomato gravy. Layer on half the eggplant slices. Top with another ½ cup gravy, then the remainder of eggplant. Finish with remaining tomato gravy. Top with Provolone cheese slices, bake 10 minutes, and serve immediately.

MELANZANE AL GAMBERI
(SHRIMP-STUFFED EGGPLANT)

Makes 8 servings

1 pound fresh shrimp, shelled and deveined (Cut large shrimp in half; leave medium shrimp whole.)
½ teaspoon salt, divided
Cayenne pepper
2 medium eggplants, stems removed and cut in half lengthwise
½ cup olive oil, divided
2 medium yellow onions, chopped
½ green bell pepper, chopped
2 cups chopped celery stalks; set celery leaves aside
2 cups stale French bread pieces, soaked in 1 cup water and squeezed dry
1½ cups plain or seasoned bread crumbs, divided
8 tablespoons butter, divided
1 teaspoon gumbo filé
1 teaspoon dried thyme leaves
2 whole bay leaves
4 tablespoons fresh chopped flat-leafed Italian parsley
4 tablespoons green onions, including tops, sliced
⅓ cup freshly grated Parmesan cheese
2 tablespoons paprika

1. Preheat oven to 350°F. Sprinkle shrimp with ¼ teaspoon salt and 1 pinch cayenne pepper and refrigerate.

2. Brush tops and bottoms of eggplants with ¼ cup olive oil and place eggplants, cut side up, in a baking pan. Bake, uncovered, until flesh is tender, about 20 minutes. Set aside to cool.

3. In a heavy skillet set over medium heat, warm remaining ¼ cup olive oil. Add onion and cook until translucent, about 3 minutes. Add bell pepper and cook until limp, about 2 minutes. Add celery and cook just until translucent, about 3 more minutes.

4. Carefully scoop out cooked eggplant pulp, leaving skins intact. Set eggplant skins aside. Chop eggplant flesh, add to cooked seasoning vegetables in the skillet, and stir over medium heat until fully incorporated. Gradually add in squeezed bread, stirring and scraping bottom of pan. Add shrimp and stir until they turn pink, about 2 minutes. Remove from heat.

5. Stir in 1 cup bread crumbs. Add 7 tablespoons butter, remaining ¼ teaspoon salt, 1 pinch cayenne pepper, filé, thyme, and bay leaves. Taste and correct the seasoning. Chop the celery leaves and add them, along with parsley and green onions. Set filling aside to cool.

6. Place eggplant shells in a buttered baking casserole. Spoon eggplant stuffing into shells. Mix together remaining ½ cup bread crumbs with Parmesan cheese and paprika. Top each eggplant with bread-crumb mixture. Dot each eggplant half with remaining 1 tablespoon butter. Bake until tops are browned, about 20 minutes. To test if fully warmed through, insert a knife in the center of eggplant and hold in place 30 seconds. If eggplant is warmed through, knife will be warm to touch. Serve immediately. Baked stuffed eggplants can be kept warm up to 15 minutes in a 200°F oven. Stuffed eggplants can be refrigerated overnight, or freeze them, then defrost and bake.

SHRIMP- OR CRAB-STUFFED MIRLITONS

Makes 12 servings

4 quarts water
1 tablespoon salt
6 mirlitons
8 tablespoons butter, divided
6 tablespoons olive oil
2 large yellow onions, chopped
1 green bell pepper, medium chopped
2 cups medium-chopped celery
2 pounds fresh shrimp, peeled and deveined, or 1 pound lump crabmeat, picked for bits of shell
2 teaspoons salt
1 teaspoon ground black pepper
1½ cups plain or seasoned bread crumbs, divided
2 bay leaves
1 teaspoon dried thyme
1 pinch cayenne pepper
1 bunch green onions, minced
2 tablespoons fresh, flat-leafed Italian parsley, minced
1 tablespoon fresh oregano, crushed
¼ cup grated Parmesan cheese
1 tablespoon paprika

1. Preheat oven to 350°F. In a large soup pot, bring water to boil. Add salt and return to a full boil. Add whole mirlitons to boiling water and cook just

until they can be pierced with a fork, about 15 minutes. Remove from water and allow to cool. Cut cooled mirlitons in half lengthwise. Remove and discard the central pit, which looks like a large almond. Use a sharp, curved knife or grapefruit spoon to remove cooked mirliton pulp from shells, being careful to keep shells intact. Set shells aside and medium chop the cooked mirliton pulp.

2. In a large, heavy skillet set over medium heat, melt 4 tablespoons butter with olive oil. Add onions and cook until translucent, about 3 minutes. Add bell pepper and cook until limp, about 2 minutes. Add celery and cook just until translucent, about 3 more minutes. Add chopped mirliton pulp and cook until mixture is dry.

3. If using shrimp, cut large ones into quarters and medium ones into halves, or leave small shrimp whole. Season shrimp or crab with salt and black pepper, add to vegetables, and cook 2 minutes. Mix in 1 cup bread crumbs, bay leaves, thyme, and cayenne. Remove from heat. Stir in green onions, parsley, and oregano. Allow to cool.

4. Remove bay leaves. Stuff mirliton dressing into reserved mirliton shells. Place stuffed mirlitons into a buttered baking casserole. Mix remaining ½ cup bread crumbs with grated Parmesan and paprika. Top each stuffed mirliton with bread-crumb mixture and dot with remaining 4 tablespoons butter. Bake until tops are brown, 20–30 minutes. Serve immediately. Baked mirlitons can be kept warm up to 15 minutes in a 200°F oven. Stuffed mirlitons can be refrigerated overnight or frozen and then defrosted and baked just before serving.

SHRIMP-STUFFED GREEN BELL PEPPERS

Makes 8 servings

1 pound fresh shrimp, shelled and deveined (Cut large shrimp in half; leave medium shrimp whole.)
Salt
Cayenne pepper
2 quarts water
4 large green peppers, cut in half lengthwise and seeds removed
½ cup olive oil
2 yellow onions, chopped
2 cups chopped celery stalks, celery leaves chopped and reserved
2 cups stale French bread, soaked in 1 cup water and squeezed dry
1½ cups plain or seasoned bread crumbs, divided
2 sticks butter, divided, plus more for greasing baking dish
1 teaspoon gumbo filé
1 teaspoon dried thyme leaves
2 whole bay leaves
4 tablespoons chopped fresh flat-leafed Italian parsley
4 tablespoons green onions, including tops, sliced
⅓ cup Parmesan cheese, grated
2 tablespoons paprika

1. Preheat oven to 350°F. Sprinkle shrimp with ¼ teaspoon salt and 1 pinch cayenne pepper. Refrigerate until needed.

2. Bring water to boil in a large pot. Add 1 tablespoon salt and return to full boil. Add green peppers to boiling water and cook until tender, about 5 minutes. Remove with a slotted spoon to drain and cool.

3. To make stuffing, in a heavy skillet, over medium heat, heat the olive oil until hot. Add onions and cook until translucent, about 3 minutes. Add celery and cook just until translucent, about 3 more minutes. Gradually add in squeezed bread, while stirring and scraping bottom of pan. Add shrimp and stir until shrimp turn pink. Remove from heat. Stir in 1 cup bread crumbs. Add 1 stick butter. Season with ¼ teaspoon salt, 1 pinch cayenne pepper, filé, thyme, and bay leaves. Taste and correct seasoning. Remove from heat. Add chopped celery leaves, parsley, and green onions. Remove bay leaves and set aside to cool slightly.

4. Evenly distribute shrimp stuffing among the bell pepper halves, mounding if necessary. Place peppers into a buttered baking casserole. Mix together remaining ½ cup bread crumbs with Parmesan cheese and paprika. Top each filled green pepper half with bread-crumb mixture and dot each with 1 tablespoon butter. Bake until tops are browned, about 30 minutes.

5. Serve immediately, or keep warm up to 15 minutes in a 200°F oven. Unbaked peppers can also be refrigerated overnight, or they can be frozen and then defrosted and baked just before serving.

FROSCIA
(SICILIAN VEGETABLE OMELET)

Makes 4–6 servings

Froscia is the ultimate leftover dish, deliciously repurposed as a nourishing, stand-alone entrée or side dish. This hearty omelet is traditionally prepared with a variety of cooked, fresh vegetables that can include florets of broccoli or cauliflower, cut green beans, fresh or canned artichoke hearts, or any variety of mixed greens.

¾ cup olive oil, divided
2 cups plain or seasoned bread crumbs, divided
3 cups fresh vegetables, blanched and thoroughly drained
Salt and pepper to taste
1 cup grated Parmesan cheese
4 large eggs
4 tablespoons fresh basil, cut into thin slices
FOR SERVING: 1 lemon, sliced into wedges, and 3 tablespoons minced fresh parsley

1. In a 12-inch shallow skillet set over medium heat, warm ½ cup of olive oil. Sprinkle 1 cup bread crumbs evenly over skillet bottom. Add vegetables, but do not stir. Sprinkle with salt and pepper and continue cooking vegetables until just warmed through. Top with cheese.

2. In a bowl, whisk eggs to a slight froth. Stir in basil. Drizzle eggs over vegetables, pouring from outer edge of skillet to the middle. Tilt the skillet to evenly distribute eggs. Reduce to low heat. Cook until eggs are set, about 3 minutes. Slide a spatula under vegetables to loosen bottom to prevent from sticking. Sprinkle remaining 1 cup bread crumbs over *froscia,* and season with salt and pepper.

3. Gently loosen *froscia* from edges and bottom of skillet. Slide onto a large plate with uncooked side up. Wipe out skillet with a paper towel.

4. Add remaining ¼ cup olive oil to skillet and warm over medium heat. Flip froscia back into the skillet with uncooked side on the bottom. Cook to brown the bread crumbs, for 1 minute. Slide *froscia* onto a warmed serving plate. *Froscia* can be kept warm up to 15 minutes, without garnish, in a 200°F oven. When ready to serve, garnish with lemon slices and fresh minced parsley. Serve immediately.

BASIC SICILIAN-STYLE TOMATO GRAVY

Makes 1 gallon

While most areas of the United States refer to this as "sauce," in Louisiana it is always called "gravy," or "red gravy."

- ½ cup olive oil
- 1 whole peeled garlic clove
- 1 large onion, chopped medium
- 4 tablespoons finely chopped green bell pepper
- 2 (6-ounce) cans tomato paste
- 1 tablespoon sugar
- 1 teaspoon cinnamon
- 1 (28-ounce) can tomato puree
- 1 (28-ounce) can crushed tomatoes
- 3 cups water
- 1 (28-ounce) can tomato sauce
- 2 teaspoons salt
- 1 teaspoon ground black pepper
- 2 cups red wine
- ½ cup chopped fresh basil, or 4 tablespoons dried
- 2 tablespoons crushed fresh oregano, or 1 tablespoon dried
- FOR SERVING: boiled pasta

1. In a large heavy saucepan, heat olive oil over medium heat. Add garlic and sauté 1 minute. Remove and discard garlic. Add onion and cook until translucent, about 5 minutes. Add bell pepper and cook until limp, about 3 more minutes.

2. Reduce heat to low and gradually stir in tomato paste. Stir in sugar and cinnamon. Stirring constantly, cook until tomato paste pulls away from the sides of the pan, about 10 minutes. Gradually stir in tomato puree and crushed tomatoes. Simmer, uncovered, 15 minutes.

3. As sauce thickens, gradually add water, one cup at a time. After all the water has been added, stir in tomato sauce, salt, and pepper. Gradually blend in wine, and continue cooking until alcohol evaporates, about 10 minutes. Add basil and oregano. Cover saucepan and simmer 45 minutes, stirring occasionally to avoid sticking.

4. Taste and correct seasonings. Serve immediately over freshly boiled pasta. Tomato gravy can be stored in the refrigerator several days and reheated as needed, or it can be frozen up to two months.

CAULIFLOWER IN TOMATO GRAVY

Makes 8–10 servings

Cauliflower in Tomato Gravy is one of those specialties served during the meatless days of Lent, and often served on the Feast of St. Joseph.

8 cups Basic Sicilian-Style Tomato Gravy (recipe page 68)
1 teaspoon salt
½ teaspoon ground black pepper
1 medium cauliflower, separated into individual flowerets, rinsed and thoroughly drained
½ cup olive oil
FOR SERVING: cooked pasta and *mudica* (recipe page 78)

1. Warm tomato gravy in a large heavy-bottomed saucepan. Mix together salt and pepper and evenly sprinkle the mixture on the cauliflower flowerets. In a heavy skillet set over medium heat, heat the olive oil. Add cauliflower, a few at a time, carefully avoiding overcrowding and breaking the flowerets. Turn to brown on all sides.

2. As cauliflower cooks, add it to the gravy. After all cauliflower is in the gravy, reduce the heat under the pot of gravy to a simmer and cook, covered, for 20 minutes. Uncover and cook, stirring occasionally, to reduce any liquid the cauliflower has released. Do so carefully to avoid breaking up flowerets, though some might break apart.

3. Remove cooked cauliflower to a serving bowl and surround with 2 cups tomato gravy. Immediately serve the bowl of cauliflower family-style on the dining table. Spoon individual servings of cauliflower over plates of freshly boiled pasta, which you might want to sauce with additional gravy. Top with *mudica*.

PASTA CON LE SARDE
(PASTA WITH SARDINES, THE TRADITIONAL ST. JOSEPH'S DAY GRAVY)

Makes 6 quarts

Pasta con le sarde is a mainstay at a St. Joseph's Day Feast. This springtime Sicilian specialty is a truly distinctive taste sensation. It melds the flavors of anchovies, or fresh sardines if available, with anise, currants, and pine nuts in a tomato gravy, which is served over anise-infused pasta and topped with *mudica,* our beloved seasoned and toasted bread crumbs.

½ cup dried currants
½ cup Marsala wine
⅓ cup olive oil
1 (2-ounce) can flat filets of anchovies packed in olive oil, or 2 ounces anchovy paste, or 2 ounces sardines
2 cups chopped fresh anise or fennel, green fronds reserved
1 gallon Basic Sicilian-Style Tomato Gravy (recipe page 68)
1 tablespoon cinnamon
Water for boiling
Salt
1 pound spaghetti
½ cup pine nuts, lightly toasted
FOR SERVING: *mudica* (recipe page 78)

1. In a small bowl, combine currants and wine and set aside. In a large heavy saucepan over medium heat, warm the olive oil. Add anchovies and mash them into the oil. Add chopped anise, and sauté 2 minutes.

2. Gradually add tomato gravy into saucepan. Stir in cinnamon and reduce heat to a simmer. Cook 15 minutes. Add soaked currants and wine and cook until wine evaporates, about 5 minutes. Remove gravy from heat.

3. Bring a large pot of salted water to a boil. Add anise greens to the boiling water and cook 5 minutes. Add pasta to the boiling anise greens and cook until pasta is just to the al dente stage, when it's cooked but still "firm to the tooth," about 6 minutes. Drain well, leaving greens mixed with the pasta.

4. When ready to serve, stir pine nuts into the warm tomato gravy. For each individual serving, top pasta with tomato gravy and a sprinkling of *mudica*. *Pasta con le sarde* gravy can be refrigerated up to 3 days, or it can be frozen up to 3 weeks.

STUFFED EGGPLANT IN TOMATO GRAVY

Makes 6–8 servings

This was another Sunday dinner specialty of my grandmother Scalise. The eggplant was always presented family-style, centered on the table in one large serving bowl.

8 cups Basic Sicilian-Style Tomato Gravy (recipe page 68)
1 large eggplant, unpeeled and stem removed
½ cup *ricotta salata, caciocavallo,* or Parmesan cheese, cut into ¼-inch wedges
2 cups freshly grated Parmesan cheese, plus additional for serving
4 tablespoons minced fresh flat-leafed Italian parsley
2 tablespoons sliced fresh basil
1 tablespoon crushed fresh oregano
1 teaspoon salt
½ teaspoon ground black pepper
½ cup olive oil
FOR SERVING: cooked pasta and freshly grated Parmesan cheese

1. Warm tomato gravy in a heavy-bottomed saucepan large enough to hold the eggplant. Set aside. With a sharp paring knife, cut 1-inch-deep slits all around the eggplant. Press cheese wedges deep into each slit.

2. Mix together grated Parmesan, parsley, basil, oregano, salt, and pepper. Stuff a pinch of this mixture into each slit, pushing it deep into the eggplant. Repeat until all the cheese mixture is pressed into the eggplant.

3. In a heavy skillet set over high heat, add the olive oil. When oil is hot, fry the stuffed eggplant well on all sides, making sure the slits are seared until they are sealed. Place whole eggplant into warmed tomato gravy. Simmer, covered, until eggplant is fully cooked, about 30 minutes. Remove cover and cook gravy on medium heat to reduce any liquid the eggplant has released.

4. Remove whole, cooked eggplant to a serving bowl and surround it with 2 cups tomato gravy. Bring the hot eggplant to the table whole. To serve, spoon individual portions of eggplant over plates of freshly boiled pasta. Sauce with additional gravy and top with freshly grated Parmesan cheese.

TOMATO GRAVY WITH HARD-BOILED EGGS

Makes 6–8 servings

Tomato gravy with hard-boiled eggs is another of those specialties typically served during the meatless days of Lent.

8 cups Basic Sicilian-Style Tomato Gravy (recipe page 68)
¼ cup olive oil
8 hard-boiled eggs, peeled
FOR SERVING: hot cooked pasta, *mudica* (recipe page 78)

1. Bring gravy to a boil in a large, heavy-bottomed saucepan. Warm the olive oil in a heavy skillet set over medium heat. Add the hard-boiled eggs to the skillet and turn to brown on all sides, carefully avoiding breaking the eggs. Gently drop eggs into the gravy, reduce heat to a simmer, and cook, covered, for 20 minutes.

2. Remove cooked eggs to a serving bowl and surround with 2 cups tomato gravy. Serve immediately family-style, bringing the whole bowl to the dining table. Spoon hard-cooked eggs over individual plates of freshly boiled pasta. Sauce with additional gravy and top with *mudica*.

CUGINA'S BREAD DOUGH

Makes 2 loaves

Every year in the weeks before St. Joseph's Day, my maternal grandmother's cousin, Cugina Nuncia Stillone Roppolo, would come to help with specialty baking for the altar. It was magical to watch her hands as she kneaded, rolled, cut, and carved dough into delectable creations. This is Cugina's bread-dough recipe.

1 package (¼ ounce) active dry yeast
2 cups warm water
1 teaspoon sugar
2 tablespoons olive oil, divided
6¼ cups all-purpose flour, divided
1 tablespoon salt
6 tablespoons lard or white vegetable shortening

1. Preheat oven to 400°F. In a medium bowl, mix yeast into warm water. Add sugar and stir until bubbles appear. Set aside.

2. Coat the inside of a large bowl with 1 tablespoon olive oil. Set aside. In another large bowl, mix together six cups flour and the salt. Add the shortening and use a fork, pastry cutter, or your fingers to blend the mixture together until it's the texture of cornmeal. Set aside.

3. Add the remaining tablespoon olive oil to the yeast mixture. Make a well in the center of the flour mixture and pour in the yeast mixture, all the while working it into the flour to form dough. If dough is too sticky to handle, add more flour, 1 tablespoon at a time. Knead dough 1 minute and place in the oiled bowl. Cover and set aside in a warm place to rise 30 minutes.

4. Punch the dough down. Separate it in half and form it into two 15-inch-long loaves. Place each loaf on a separate ungreased baking sheet. Bake until loaves are golden brown, about 20 minutes.

ST. JOSEPH'S DAY BREAD

Makes 2 braided loaves

1 tablespoon olive oil
2 (¼-ounce) packages active dry yeast
3 cups warm water, divided
2 tablespoons sugar, divided
7½ cups all-purpose flour, divided
½ cup lard or white vegetable shortening
2 tablespoons Mediterranean Sea salt
1 egg, slightly beaten
½ cup unhulled sesame seeds

1. Lightly grease two flat baking sheets and a large bowl with the olive oil. Set them aside. In a small bowl, sprinkle yeast over ½ cup warm water. Stir well. Add 1 tablespoon sugar and set aside until bubbles develop, about 5 minutes. In a large bowl, use a pastry blender, a fork, or your fingers to mix together 7 cups flour and shortening until it's the texture of cornmeal. Set aside.

2. In a separate bowl, mix together the remaining 2½ cups warm water, remaining tablespoon sugar, and the salt. Make a well in the flour mixture and pour in the salted water. Mix to form a sticky dough. Add yeast mixture into

the dough and knead to fully incorporate. Add more flour, ¼ cup at a time, as needed to form a smooth dough. Form the dough into a smooth ball. Place it in the large oiled bowl. Let it stand 5 minutes, then knead again 1 minute.

3. Separate dough in half. To shape into braided loaves, roll each half of dough into a rope, approximately 30 inches long. Cut each rope into three pieces and braid them into a loaf, folding under and pinching the ends to secure the braid. Place each braided loaf onto one of the prepared baking sheets. Cover with a dry cloth and set aside until doubled in size, about 50 minutes.

4. About 20 minutes before you're ready to bake, preheat your oven to 400°F. Brush tops and sides of bread with beaten egg. Sprinkle on sesame seeds. Bake until golden brown, about 20 minutes. Serve immediately. Loaves can be rewarmed in a 350°F oven for 5–10 minutes.

BRUSCHETTA

Makes about 12 servings

A day-old French baguette or Italian bread loaf
½ cup extra virgin olive oil
2 tablespoons dried oregano
1 teaspoon ground black pepper
½ cup freshly grated Parmesan cheese

1. Preheat oven to 350°F. If using a baguette, cut ¼-inch slices on a 45° angle. For Italian bread, cut ¼-inch slices on a 45° angle, then cut each piece into quarters, approximately 1–2 inches each.

2. Place bread slices on a baking sheet, and brush the tops with olive oil. Sprinkle with oregano and black pepper. Top with Parmesan cheese. (At this point, the bread slices can be set aside at room temperature up to 30 minutes.)

3. Bake just until cheese melts, about 10 minutes. Serve immediately.

SCHIACCIATA
(“PRESSED” FLATBREAD)

Makes two 16×13×1½-inch pans

This rustic pan bread was a specialty that my grandmother Scalise always served with Sunday dinner. *Schiacciata* literally means “pressed,” which is what you do to the dough with your fingers before you let it rise.

¾ cup olive oil, divided
1 unbaked recipe Cugina’s Bread Dough (page 73), separated into two equal dough balls
2 cups chopped yellow onion
1 (28-ounce) can whole tomatoes, drained, broken into bits
4 tablespoons sliced fresh basil or 2 tablespoons dried basil
2 tablespoons crushed fresh oregano or 4 teaspoons dried
2 teaspoons ground black pepper
2 cups shaved Parmesan cheese

1. Brush bottoms and sides of two 16×13×1½-inch pans with 2 tablespoons olive oil each. Place a dough ball into the center of each pan and press with your fingertips to stretch and fill the entire bottoms of the pans.

2. Evenly sprinkle one cup onion over the dough in each pan and press them directly in. Divide drained tomatoes between the pans and press directly into dough, spacing evenly. Divide the basil and oregano between the pans and press directly into dough, spacing evenly. In each pan, evenly sprinkle on 1 teaspoon black pepper and drizzle on ¼ cup olive oil.

3. Cover each pan with parchment paper or foil. Set aside in a warm place and allow to rise 1 hour.

4. Preheat oven to 375°F. Remove parchment paper from the pans and bake bread 15 minutes. Remove from oven and lightly sprinkle 1 cup Parmesan over each loaf. Bake until the tops are lightly browned, another 5 minutes. Cut into squares and serve immediately. Baked *schiacciata* can be refrigerated and rewarmed 5–10 minutes in a 350°F oven, or it can be served cold.

SFINGIONI
(SICILIAN PIZZA)

Makes two 16×13×1½-inch pans

This recipe was given to me by my dear friend Virginia Muscarello Patechek, and it is prepared as she learned from her mother, Lena Bentivegna Muscarello.

½ cup olive oil, divided
1 unbaked recipe Cugina's Bread Dough (page 73), separated into two equal dough balls
1 (2-ounce) can flat fillets of anchovies packed in olive oil
1 cup Parmesan cheese cubes, cut ¼ inch
1¼ cups grated Parmesan cheese
½ cup seasoned bread crumbs
4 tablespoons sliced fresh basil or 2 tablespoons dried
2 tablespoons crushed fresh oregano or 6 teaspoons dried
2 teaspoons black pepper

1. Brush bottoms and sides of two, 16×13×1½-inch pans with 2 tablespoons olive oil each. Place a dough ball in center of each pan. Press dough with fingertips to stretch and fill entire bottoms of the pans.

2. Drain and discard olive oil from anchovies and cut them into ¼ inch bits. Divide anchovies between pans and use fingertips to press them into the dough, spacing evenly. In each pan, evenly space ½ cup Parmesan cheese cubes and press it into the dough.

3. Combine grated Parmesan, bread crumbs, basil, oregano, and black pepper. Sprinkle mixture evenly over dough in each pan. In each pan, drizzle 2 tablespoons olive oil over bread-crumb mixture. Cover pans with parchment paper or a dry cloth and set aside in a warm place to rise 1 hour.

4. Preheat oven to 375°F. Remove parchment paper from the pans and bake bread until tops and bottoms are lightly browned, 20 minutes. Cut into squares and serve immediately. Baked *sfingioni* can be refrigerated and rewarmed 5–10 minutes in a 350°F oven, or served cold.

MUDICA
(SEASONED BREAD CRUMBS)

Makes 6 cups

Sprinkled over the traditional *pasta con le sarde,* these tasty bread crumbs are said to symbolize the sawdust of St. Joseph's carpentry workshop.

6 cups torn pieces of day-old Italian bread
1 cup olive oil
2 tablespoons granulated sugar
2 teaspoons black pepper

1. Lightly toast bread. In a blender or food processor, process toasted bread to a medium crumb texture. Refrigerate until needed.

2. In a large heavy skillet set over medium heat, warm the olive oil. Sprinkle bread crumbs over the olive oil and stir with a wooden spoon to coat evenly. Stirring constantly, gradually add sugar and continue stirring and toasting until bread crumbs are golden brown. Stir in black pepper. Remove skillet from heat.

3. Transfer *mudica* to a glass jar or bowl. Allow to cool to room temperature. Keeps in tightly covered jars up to 1 week.

4. *Mudica* is best served warm. To rewarm *mudica,* place it in a microwave-safe bowl and cook on full power 30 seconds. If not completely warmed through, stir and return to the microwave for an additional 30 seconds. To serve, bring a bowl of warmed *mudica* to the table as a topping for pasta.

7

St. Joseph Altar Confections

Each St. Joseph Altar displays an ambrosial assemblage of confections, cakes, cookies, and hand-carved pastries that represent sacred symbols. With Sicily's and Louisiana's shared love of sugar, it was fated that these recipes for sweets would become the essentials of traditional St. Joseph Altar delicacies. For all those who lovingly prepare these specialties, they can be assured of the blessedness of their craft, as St. Joseph is a patron of pastry chefs.

Photo by Anthony "Chopper" Leone.

CANNOLI

Makes 16

Everyone's favorite Sicilian confection, these homemade tube-shaped shells are well worth the effort and are best appreciated after participating in a multigenerational "cannoli-rolling" party. In this recipe I give ingredients and instructions for chocolate and lemon fillings. Each shell is filled with a portion of both, creating a traditional treat bursting with flavor.

Cannoli Shells

SPECIAL EQUIPMENT: twelve 5-inch-long stainless-steel cannoli tubes and a pasta machine

2 quarts vegetable oil
1 cup all-purpose flour
1 tablespoon granulated sugar
1 tablespoon olive oil
2 tablespoons Marsala wine, warmed
2 tablespoons warm water
1 egg white, slightly beaten

1. Dip the cannoli tubes in room temperature cooking oil. Drain off excess oil and set tubes aside.

2. In a small bowl combine the flour and sugar. Stir in the tablespoon of olive oil and mix to the texture of cornmeal. Combine the Marsala and water, and stir into the flour mixture until it is a stiff, but workable, dough. Knead dough until elastic, about 1 minute. Cover and set aside 10 minutes. Separate dough into 4 pieces and keep them covered until ready to use.

3. Working with one piece of dough at a time, use the pasta machine to roll them out into ⅛-inch-thick strips, approximately 4 inches wide by 12 inches long. Lay the sheets of dough on a lightly floured surface. Using a 4-inch-diameter saucer or bowl as a guide, cut out 4 circles from each dough sheet.

4. Center the cannoli tubes on the dough circles. Both ends of the metal tubes should extend beyond the dough edges by ½ inch. Fold the dough circles over the tubes and seal the center of the overlap with the beaten egg white. Be careful to avoid getting egg white on the tube.

5. When ready to fry, heat the 2 quarts oil in a deep fryer to 360°F. To test if the oil is ready, drop in a small piece of dough. If it floats to the top, the oil is hot enough. Fry cannoli shells on the metal tubes until golden, 2–3 minutes. Drain on paper towels and allow to cool slightly.

6. Using a clean, dry cloth, firmly hold the cannoli shells and gently push the metal tubes through. Set shells aside until ready to fill. Once fully cooled, unfilled cannoli shells can be stored in an airtight container at room temperature up to 1 week, or frozen up to 3 weeks.

Chocolate Cannoli Filling

Makes enough to fill half of 16 cannoli

1 pound (16 ounces) ricotta, preferably fresh (recipe page 115), or thoroughly drained commercial ricotta
½ cup powdered sugar
1 tablespoon unsweetened cocoa
½ cup semisweet chocolate mini-morsels
1 teaspoon ground cinnamon
½ teaspoon freshly grated nutmeg
1 tablespoon pure vanilla extract
2 tablespoons Frangelico liqueur or brandy

Lemon Cannoli Filling

Makes enough to fill half of 16 cannoli

1 pound (16 ounces) ricotta, preferably fresh (recipe page 115), or thoroughly drained commercial ricotta
½ cup powdered sugar
2 tablespoons honey
1 tablespoon lemon juice
1 teaspoon lemon zest
¼ cup candied citron, medium chopped
¼ teaspoon freshly grated nutmeg
¼ teaspoon almond extract
1 tablespoon Amaretto liqueur or brandy

Prepare fillings in separate bowls. In the order given, gently fold ingredients into ricotta cheese. Refrigerate the bowls of filling at least 20 minutes. Ricotta filling is extremely fragile, so use it within 1 day. It can be frozen up to 3 weeks.

Cannoli Assembly

Cooled cannoli shells
Chocolate and lemon fillings
½ cup powdered sugar

Use a long-handled spoon or a pastry bag to stuff the shells with the fillings. Beginning from the centers, fill half of each cannoli shell with one of the fillings. Do the same on the other side with the other filling. Dust the filled shells with powdered sugar and serve immediately. Cannoli are best when they are filled just before serving. You can fill them in advance and freeze up to 3 weeks. If frozen, let them sit at room temperature 20 minutes and dust with powdered sugar just before serving.

Photo by Anthony "Chopper" Leone.

SFINGE DI SAN GIUSEPPE
(ST. JOSEPH'S DAY CREAM PUFFS)

Makes 36–48

This recipe has been passed down through generations of the Brocato family, which owns Brocato's Italian Ice Cream and Pastry store on North Carrollton Avenue in New Orleans. It was given to me by Arthur Brocato, grandson of Angelo Brocato Sr., Brocato's founder. If you visit Brocato's on St. Joseph's Day, you are in for a special treat. Not only can you taste specialties made from recipes Angelo brought from Sicily over 100 years ago, but you can also view their St. Joseph Altar on display in the store during the week celebrating San Giuseppe's Feast. Be sure to order the *sfinge di San Giuseppe,* a filled cream puff-type pastry made fresh in-house and available only on the days closest to St. Joseph's feast day.

Sfinge Filling

3½ pounds fresh ricotta (recipe page 115), or thoroughly drained commercial ricotta
2¾ cups granulated sugar
⅛ teaspoon ground cinnamon
4–6 ounces mini chocolate chips
4 ounces chopped candied citron

Place ricotta in a large bowl and fold in sugar by hand, or use low speed with a mixer. Do not beat on high speed or mixture will become too soft. Mix in the cinnamon. Use a spoon to gently fold in chocolate chips and citron. Refrigerate at least two hours before using.

Sfinge Pastry Shells

2 quarts vegetable oil for frying
2 cups water
4 tablespoons white vegetable shortening or lard
4½ cups cake flour or all-purpose flour
1 teaspoon salt
12 large eggs

1. Preheat oil in a deep fryer or a large, deep pot to 350°F. Meanwhile, over medium-high heat, combine water and shortening in a 2- or 3-quart pot. Completely melt the shortening and bring the mixture to a full boil. Remove pot from the heat, immediately add flour and salt, and use a wooden spoon to mix thoroughly.

2. Place warm dough in the bowl of a standing electric mixer with a flat beater attachment and turn the mixer on low speed. Add eggs one at a time and mix until well blended.

3. Drop batter into heated oil using a 1½-inch ice cream scoop or heaping tablespoonsful. As they cook, *sfinge* will expand into shells, become hollow in the center, and turn themselves over, so don't overcrowd the fryer. Remove when golden brown, drain on paper towels, and allow to cool. Unfilled shells can be stored in a covered container in the refrigerator 1–2 days.

Sfinge Assembly

Sfinge Pastry Shells
Sfinge Filling
36–48 candied cherries or strips of candied orange peel
1 cup powdered sugar

To make a well for the filling, use a small knife to cut an opening through the top center of each fried *sfinge* shell, hallowing out a hole down to the middle of the pastry. Use a pastry bag or spoon to fill each shell with Sfinge Filling. Garnish the tops with a candied cherry or a strip of candied orange peel. Sprinkle lightly with powdered sugar and serve immediately.

CASSATEDI
(FRIED RICOTTA-FILLED RAVIOLI)

Makes eight 6-inch or twelve 4-inch cassatedi

This sweet, crescent-shaped fried ravioli was a specialty of my maternal grandmother's sister, my great-aunt Annie Caronna Ricca, who always prepared *cassatedi* for breakfast on St. Joseph's Day.

⅓ cup cornstarch
2¼ cups all-purpose flour, divided
2 large eggs
1 tablespoon olive oil
2–3 tablespoons warm water
2 quarts vegetable oil
Cassatedi Filling (recipe follows)
1 egg white, whisked to a light froth

1. Cover the bottom of a sheet pan with parchment paper and lightly brush on cornstarch. Set aside. Sift 2 cups flour into a shallow bowl. In another bowl, lightly beat the eggs and stir in olive oil. Gradually add egg mixture into the flour, mixing lightly until fully incorporated. Make a well in the center of the dough and add water one tablespoon at a time, using only as much as needed to form a smooth paste. If dough becomes too sticky to handle, sprinkle in just enough flour to make it pliable.

2. Separate dough into two balls. Knead each ball until smooth, about 5 minutes, then return them to the bowl. Cover bowl with a damp cloth and allow to rest 15 minutes.

3. Working with one dough ball at a time, knead dough again 1 minute. On a lightly floured surface, roll dough to ⅛ inch thick and stretch it to a 10-inch square. Press a bowl or saucer onto rolled-out pastry to form rounds of desired size, usually 4 inches for small *cassatedi* or 6 inches for large. Cut the rounds close together but do not overlap. Use a fluted pastry wheel to cut out each circle. Brush the circles lightly with cornstarch, place them on the sheet pan, and cover with a dry cloth or parchment paper.

4. Heat cooking oil in a deep fryer to 360°F. Working with one circle of dough at a time, spoon *cassatedi* filling into the center of the dough, 1 tablespoon for small *cassateda,* or 2 tablespoons for large. Lightly brush egg white

along edges of circle. To seal *cassateda,* flip top half of circle over the ricotta filling to form a half-moon shape, being careful that all filling is contained inside. Using the back of a small-tined fork, press around the entire open edge, making sure to seal from corner to corner.

5. To test if oil is ready, drop in a small piece of dough. When dough rises to the top, oil is ready to fry. Add several *cassatedi* into fryer, carefully avoiding overcrowding to prevent them from sticking and tearing. Fry until golden brown and remove to drain on paper towels. While still hot, shake on powdered sugar and serve immediately.

6. If storing filled, uncooked *cassatedi* in your refrigerator or freezer, brush each with a light coating of cornstarch. Uncooked *cassatedi* can be refrigerated overnight. For longer storage, individually wrap *cassatedi,* put them in sealed plastic food-storage bags, and put in your freezer up to 2 weeks. Frozen *cassatedi* should be thoroughly thawed before frying, preferably overnight in your refrigerator.

Cassatedi Filling

1 cup ricotta, preferably fresh (recipe page 115), or thoroughly drained commercial ricotta
⅓ cup powdered sugar, plus more for sprinkling
2 tablespoons honey
1 tablespoon grated lemon zest
2 tablespoons minced fresh parsley
2 teaspoons freshly grated nutmeg

Place ricotta in a large bowl and stir in ⅓ cup powdered sugar. Gently blend in honey and lemon zest. Stir in parsley and nutmeg and set aside.

CICEROTTI
(FRIED DESSERT RAVIOLI WITH CHESTNUTS OR CHICKPEAS)

Makes 3 dozen

These delicious fried ravioli are the holiday dessert specialty of my dear friend Rosa Ricciardi.

SPECIAL EQUIPMENT: *a pasta machine*

- 6 cups all-purpose flour
- ½ cup vegetable oil, plus 2 quarts for frying
- 1 large egg
- 1 tablespoon ground cinnamon
- 1 pinch of salt
- 1 bottle (750 mL) Pinot Grigio wine, warmed
- Cicerotti Filling (recipe follows)
- FOR SERVING: ½ cup warmed honey

1. To make ravioli, in a bowl mix together flour, ½ cup vegetable oil, egg, cinnamon, and salt. Make a well in the center, pour in the wine, and mix fully. Knead into a smooth dough, about 2–5 minutes. Cover dough and set aside at least 30 minutes, or until ready to roll out and fill, up to 2 hours.

2. Divide dough into 12 pieces and keep the ones you are not working with covered with plastic wrap. As you work with each piece, divide it in half, flatten the halves into rough rectangles, and roll them through a pasta machine until they are approximately ⅛ inch thick. Roll each piece into 3×12-inch strips. Place the two dough strips, one above the other, on a dry work surface. Onto the bottom strip, space 6 mounds of Cicerotti Filling (1 teaspoon each) about 2 inches apart. Cover with remaining dough strip. With a fluted wheel or ravioli stamp, cut into individual ravioli squares. To seal, press edges with a small-tined fork. Place filled *cicerotti* on a baking sheet, cover with a dry cloth, and set aside. Continue until all dough is filled.

3. When ready to fry, preheat the 2 quarts oil in a fryer to 325°F. Drop small batches of filled *cicerotti* into heated oil and fry, turning once, until they rise to the top and are light gold. Drain on paper towels. Fried *cicerotti* can be kept warm up to 20 minutes in a 200°F oven.

4. Just before serving, transfer warm *cicerotti* onto a decorative platter, drizzle with warm honey, and serve immediately. Before they are fried, *cicerotti* can be frozen in sealed food-storage bags up to 3 weeks. Defrost frozen *cicerotti* fully before frying.

Cicerotti Filling

- 5 pounds chestnuts, roasted and peeled (yields approximately 4 cups) or 4 cups chickpeas, cooked 20 minutes in plain boiling water and drained
- 1½ cups granulated sugar
- 4 (6-ounce) bars Hershey's Milk Chocolate, grated
- 6 ounces sweetened cocoa powder
- 3 tablespoons ground cinnamon
- 1 tablespoon allspice
- ½ teaspoon ground cloves
- 1 (4-ounce) package chopped citron
- 4 tablespoons pure vanilla extract
- 4 tablespoons Amaretto liqueur
- Juice of 2 oranges (for chestnut filling only)
- 4 ounces brewed espresso coffee (for chestnut filling only)

In a food processor or blender, puree chestnuts or boiled chickpeas. Remove to a bowl. Add in sugar, Hershey's chocolate, cocoa, cinnamon, allspice, and cloves. Fold in citron. Stir in vanilla and Amaretto. If using chestnuts, add orange juice and espresso. Mixture should be the consistency of mashed potatoes. Cover and refrigerate overnight. Mixture can be frozen up to 2 weeks. If frozen, defrost completely at room temperature before filling the ravioli.

CARTAS
(HONEY WHEELS)

Makes 16 pastries

These are Sicilian confections of simple fried dough shaped into circles and dipped in warm honey. Honey wheels are a splendid representative of Sicilian pastry art, and a delicious accompaniment to a cup of espresso or a serving of lemon ice.

2 tablespoons Marsala wine, warmed
2 tablespoons warm water
1 cup all-purpose flour
1 tablespoon sugar
1 tablespoon olive oil
1 egg white, slightly beaten
2 quarts vegetable oil
½ cup honey
Zest of 1 lemon, grated

1. Combine Marsala and water in a small bowl and set aside. In a larger bowl, mix together flour and sugar. Using a fork, mix in the olive oil until the mixture is the texture of cornmeal. Gradually stir in wine mixture to form a stiff but workable dough. Knead dough until elastic, about 1 minute. Cover and set aside 10 minutes.

Photo by Anthony "Chopper" Leone.

2. Separate dough into four pieces. Work with one piece of dough at a time and keep the remainder covered. Roll a piece of dough into a rectangle that's at least 8×4 inches. It should be ⅛ inch thick. Using a fluted pastry wheel, cut dough sheet into four 2×4-inch strips.

3. To form *cartas,* gently fold the pastry strips in half lengthwise, with the fluted edges meeting and facing up. Pinch the left end of the folded strip and seal the pinched edge with egg white. This is the center of the *carta*. Gently coil the folded dough around the center into the shape of a spiraled wheel. Finish by folding the end of the dough strip under the wheel, and seal it with egg white.

4. Heat vegetable oil in a deep fryer to 360°F. To test if it's hot enough, drop in a small piece of dough, and when it floats to the top, the oil is ready. Fry a few at a time just until they're golden, but not browned. Drain on paper towels and set aside to cool.

5. When ready to serve, heat honey in a small skillet just to a simmer. Dip fried *cartas* into honey, turning to fully coat. Remove to a wire rack to drain. Top each with a sprinkling of grated lemon zest and serve immediately. Cooled, fried *cartas* (without the honey and lemon zest) can be stored in a dry container up to 1 week, or frozen in a sealed container up to 3 weeks.

PIGNOLATI
(FRIED AND SUGARED PASTRY MOUNDS)

Makes 6–8 large or 36 bite-sized mounds

In some Sicilian dialects *pignolati* are called *gigis,* and in Northern Italy they are known as *struffoli.* Using just three basic ingredients, these sugar-coated bits of fried pasta dough are magically transformed into celebratory confections that are Italian favorites for Christmas, Easter, and St. Joseph's Day. Mounded into pyramid shapes, they are said to represent pine cones, the simple toys of the Child Jesus. Making *pignolati* is truly one of those labor-of-love projects.

1 quart, plus 1 tablespoon vegetable oil
1–1¼ cups all-purpose flour, divided
2 eggs, beaten
1 cup sugar, divided

1. In a deep pot or electric fryer, heat 1 quart vegetable oil to 375°F. With 1 tablespoon vegetable oil, lightly grease a shallow baking pan and thoroughly coat insides of 4 teacups. Set aside.

2. In a shallow bowl, add 1 cup flour and stir in eggs, mixing to form dough. If dough is too sticky to handle, add more flour. Knead dough 1 minute and separate into 2 balls. Place dough balls into a bowl, cover, and set aside 10 minutes.

Photo by Anthony "Chopper" Leone.

3. Take 3 tablespoons of dough at a time and roll it into a 1×12-inch-long pencil-like strip. On a 45-degree angle, cut each dough strip into ½-inch pieces. Set dough pieces on a floured linen towel and keep covered with another linen towel. Repeat the process until all the dough has been rolled and cut.

4. Drop one cup of cut dough pieces at a time into the hot oil. Stirring to keep pieces from sticking together, fry until light golden. Drain on paper towels and set aside. Continue until all dough pieces are fried. After fully cooled and before they are sugared, fried *pignolati* pieces can be stored in airtight tins and kept in a cool, dry place up to 1 week.

5. To sugarcoat *pignolati,* in a heavy skillet over medium heat, add ½ cup sugar and stir with a wooden spoon until sugar has melted into a thin, light golden-colored syrup. Reduce heat to a simmer and gradually add 3 cups of fried dough into the hot syrup. Stir until pieces are completely coated. Spoon sugared pieces into the greased baking pan.

6. To form *pignolati* into pine-cone shaped mounds, use a wooden spoon to pack sugared *pignolati* into greased teacups. Allow to set several minutes, then remove from cups and work quickly with hands to form into mounds. Set aside to cool completely. Add remaining sugar to skillet and repeat process until all fried dough pieces have been sugared and formed.

7. To form small, bite-sized mounds, work quickly with a wooden spoon and press together 3 sugared *pignolati* pieces. Allow to set several minutes then set aside to cool completely. When thoroughly cooled, bite-sized sugared *pignolati* can be placed into waxed soufflé cups or mini foil cupcake liners. Bite-sized *pignolati* mounds and large *pignolati* can be sealed in plastic wrap and airtight tins and kept in a cool, dry place up to 1 week.

PIGNOCCATA
(SUGAR- AND HONEY-COATED FRIED PASTRY MOUNDS)

Makes 6–8

Pignoccata is another version of the sugared, fried dough known as *pignolati*. This recipe is from Chef Giuseppe Troia, whose home is the seaport town of Carini in the province of Palermo. Chef Troia is a *primo pasticcere,* first pastry chef, who perfected his artistry through studies at the Accademia Etoile di Sottomarina. Recognized as a master of classic Sicilian pastries and confections, Chef Troia reminds us that *pignoccata* is one of those Sicilian specialties rarely seen outside of homes and typically reserved for family celebrations.

1½–2 cups all-purpose flour, plus additional for sprinkling
1 pinch salt
2 large eggs, lightly fork-beaten to a froth
1 quart, plus 1 tablespoon vegetable oil
1 cup granulated sugar, divided
½ cup honey, preferably orange-blossom honey, divided
Zest of half a lemon, divided
Zest of half an orange, divided

1. In a shallow bowl, add 1½ cups flour and salt. Gradually stir in beaten eggs to form a dough. If dough is too sticky to handle, gradually sprinkle in more flour. Knead dough until it's smooth, about 3 minutes. Cover with a linen towel and set aside 10 minutes.

2. Sprinkle flour on a linen towel and set it aside. Working with 4 tablespoons of dough at a time, roll it into 1×12-inch-long pencil-like strips. Cutting on a 45-degree angle, slice each dough strip into ½-inch pieces. Lay cut pieces on the floured towel, and keep covered with another linen towel. Repeat the process until all the dough has been rolled and cut.

3. In a large, heavy-bottomed pot or deep fryer, heat 1 quart vegetable oil to 375°F. With the remaining 1 tablespoon oil, lightly grease the bottom of a shallow baking pan and thoroughly coat the insides of 4 teacups. Set aside.

4. Use a slotted spoon to drop only one cup of cut dough pieces in the heated oil at a time. Fry until pieces rise to the top and are light golden. Drain on paper towels. After they are fully cooled and before they are sugared, you can seal the fried dough pieces in plastic storage bags or tightly covered tins up to 1 week.

5. To sugarcoat *pignoccata,* in a heavy skillet set over medium heat, add ½ cup sugar and stir with a wooden spoon until sugar is melted and turns into a thin, light golden syrup. Add ¼ cup honey and half the lemon and orange zests and stir until completely infused. Reduce heat to a simmer and add 2 cups of fried dough into the syrup. Stir until dough pieces are completely coated. Turn the skillet of sugared pieces onto the greased baking pan, then pack them into the oiled cups. Allow *pignoccata* mounds to set several minutes. Remove them from the cups and work quickly with your hands to form mounds. Set aside to cool.

6. Melt remaining ½ cup sugar in the skillet, add remaining ¼ cup honey and zests, and repeat the coating process with the remaining dough balls. *Pignoccata* can be stored in air-tight tins and kept in a cool, dry place up to 1 week.

CRISPELLE DI SAN GIUSEPPE
(SWEET FRIED RICE BALLS)

Makes 2 dozen (Begin early in the day or the day before.)

¼ cup golden raisins
2 tablespoons Marsala wine
1 fresh lemon
1 fresh orange
2½ cups whole milk, divided
¾ cup granulated sugar, divided
1 pinch salt
½ cup uncooked Arborio rice
2 (¼-ounce) packets active dry yeast
2 large eggs, separated
1½–2 cups all-purpose flour, divided
2 quarts vegetable oil
1 tablespoon ground cinnamon

1. In a microwave-safe bowl, warm together raisins and wine 30 seconds. Set aside.

2. Use a potato peeler to carefully remove the rinds from the lemon and the orange, avoiding the white pith. Set the rinds aside and save the lemon and orange for another use. In a medium, heavy-bottomed saucepan, add citrus rinds, 2¼ cups milk, ½ cup sugar, and salt. Cook over medium heat until sugar dissolves, about 3 minutes. Stir in the rice and bring to a boil. Lower heat to medium and cook, uncovered, 15 minutes.

3. Remove and discard citrus rinds. Reduce heat to a simmer. Stirring constantly with a wooden spoon, cook until milk is absorbed and rice becomes creamy, an additional 5 minutes. Remove from heat and add the raisins and Marsala. Cool to room temperature, then refrigerate several hours and up to overnight.

4. Before mixing batter, remove rice mixture from the refrigerator and set it aside until it comes to room temperature, about 30 minutes. Heat remaining ¼ cup milk to lukewarm. Add yeast to a medium bowl, stir in the warm milk, and set aside 10 minutes. Beat egg yolks with an electric mixer until doubled in volume. Stir into yeast mixture.

5. Add 1 cup flour to a large bowl. Stir in the egg yolk mixture until it's fully incorporated. Add rice mixture to flour mixture. Beat egg whites until stiff and gently fold them into the rice-flour mixture. Cover and set aside to rise, about 6–8 hours.

6. When ready to fry, preheat oil in a deep fryer or a large, deep pot to 325°F. Pour ½ cup flour onto a sheet pan. Using 2 tablespoons at a time, hand-roll the batter into 2-inch balls. If the batter is too sticky to handle, add ½ cup flour and mix until smooth. Lightly dredge *crispelle* balls in the flour on the sheet pan. Set aside on parchment paper or foil.

7. When oil is hot, fry *crispelle* until they float and are golden brown all over. Drain on paper towels. Mix remaining ¼ cup sugar with cinnamon. Roll hot *crispelle* in cinnamon mixture and serve immediately.

AMARETTI
(ALMOND MERINGUES)

Makes 3 dozen

Whites of 2 large eggs
8 ounces blanched whole almonds, divided
¾ cup (12 tablespoons) granulated sugar, divided
¼ teaspoon cream of tartar
¼ teaspoon almond extract

1. Preheat oven to 300°F. Put egg whites in a large mixing bowl and let them stand at room temperature 30 minutes. Meanwhile, line 2 baking sheets with parchment paper or nonstick foil. Set aside.

2. In a food processor or blender, process the almonds with 4 tablespoons sugar until almonds are finely ground. Do not overgrind, or the nuts will quickly turn to paste. Set the ground almonds aside.

Photo by Cynthia LeJeune Nobles.

3. Add the cream of tartar and almond extract to the egg whites. Beat with an electric mixer on medium speed until soft peaks form. Gradually add the remaining 8 tablespoons sugar, one tablespoon at a time, beating on high speed until stiff peaks form and sugar is dissolved. Fold in 7 ounces ground almonds.

4. Use rounded teaspoons to drop meringue mixture onto the prepared baking sheets, spacing about 1½ inches apart. Evenly distribute a sprinkling of remaining ground almonds over each meringue. Bake just until cookies begin to brown, 12–15 minutes. Centers will be soft. Turn oven heat off. Allow cookies to dry in the oven with the door closed for 30 minutes.

5. Carefully peel cookies from parchment paper. *Amaretti* can be stored up to one week in an airtight container kept in a cool, dry place.

ORANGE-CHOCOLATE MERINGUES

Makes 36

Each sweet bite of these meringues is infused with flavors of citrus, vanilla, and chocolate. They remind me of Venetian-style glazed orange slices dipped in rich, dark chocolate.

Whites from 2 large eggs, room temperature
⅔ cup granulated white sugar
1 pinch salt
1 teaspoon pure vanilla extract
¼ teaspoon King Arthur brand Fiori di Sicilia flavoring
1 package (6 ounces) mini semisweet chocolate bits
4 teaspoons chocolate or orange-colored sprinkles

1. Preheat oven to 375°F. Line a baking sheet with nonstick foil or parchment paper.

2. Beat egg whites until stiff, but not completely dry. Gradually add sugar, continuing to beat until sugar is fully incorporated, about 5 minutes. Add salt, vanilla, and Fiori di Sicilia flavoring, continuing to beat 1 minute. Fold in chocolate bits.

3. Drop mixture by teaspoonfuls onto prepared cookie sheet, spacing about 1 inch apart. Lightly coat the top of each meringue with sprinkles. Place meringues in preheated oven and turn the oven heat off. Leave meringues in 15 minutes, then turn oven to 350°F. Leave meringues in an additional 5 minutes, or until they are fully dried. Meringues will develop a creamy toasted color. (You can also place them into the preheated oven, turn oven heat off, and leave the meringues in the oven overnight.)

4. Allow meringues to cool thoroughly on the baking sheet. When they are cool, carefully remove them from the foil. Meringues should be kept in a cool, dry place. If packaged in sealed tins or plastic bags, they can be stored at room temperature in a dry place up to 1 week.

CHOCOLATE WINE BISCOTTI

Makes 12 dozen

1 cup golden raisins
1 cup Marsala wine
4 large eggs
2 cups granulated sugar
1 cup white vegetable shortening
7 cups all-purpose flour
½ cup cocoa powder
2 tablespoons ground cinnamon
5 teaspoons baking powder
2 teaspoons allspice
1 teaspoon nutmeg
1 cup chopped pecans or walnuts
5 tablespoons milk
2 cups powdered sugar
4 drops oil of anise
1 drop red food coloring

1. Preheat oven to 350°F. Place raisins and wine in a small bowl and set aside. In a medium bowl, use medium mixer speed to beat eggs to a light froth, about 2 minutes. Gradually beat in sugar. Blend in shortening and set aside.

2. In a large bowl, sift together flour, cocoa, cinnamon, baking powder, allspice, and nutmeg. Stir to thoroughly blend. Stir in chopped nuts. Gently stir the egg and shortening mixture into the flour mixture. When fully combined, fold in raisin-and-wine mixture.

3. Knead dough 3 minutes and separate into 3 equal portions. Place the dough pieces in a large bowl, cover, and set aside 10 minutes. Working with 1 portion of dough at a time, pinch off 1¼-inch pieces of dough, or scoop out pieces with the large side of a melon-ball cutter. Hand-roll each piece into a ½-inch ball. Place cookie balls about 2 inches apart on ungreased baking sheets. Pat each ball to slightly flatten. Bake until bottoms are slightly brown, about 20 minutes. Remove from oven and let cool thoroughly on a rack.

4. When ready for icing, gradually blend milk into powdered sugar, one tablespoon at a time, until you have a smooth, slightly runny paste. Add anise and food coloring. The icing should be a delicate pink. In a large bowl, add half of the cooled cookies. Pour all the icing over cookies and mix lightly with a wooden spoon or spatula to thoroughly coat each. With a slotted spoon carefully place cookies onto baking racks to dry, spacing apart to avoid touching. Add remaining cooled cookies to the icing in the bowl and repeat procedure. Allow cookies to dry completely before packaging. Chocolate Wine Biscotti can be sealed in tins and stored at room temperature in a dry place up to 2 weeks, or they can be frozen up to 2 months.

Photo by Anthony "Chopper" Leone.

ANISE COOKIES

Makes 2 dozen

The hands of my grandmother Accardo were always busy with knitting, crocheting, or baking delicious confections. These are the cookies my daughter Jeanne, who was then three years old, asked for on a visit: "I want one of those cookies Mommie knits."

2 tablespoons vegetable shortening
2 large eggs, at room temperature
1 cup granulated sugar
1½ cups all-purpose flour, measured after sifting
3 drops anise oil
Nonpareil sprinkles

1. Thoroughly grease two cookie sheets with the vegetable shortening. Set aside. In a large bowl and with an electric mixer on highest speed, beat eggs until doubled in volume and light lemon colored, about 8 minutes. Gradually add sugar while continually beating an additional 8 minutes. Reduce speed to low. While continually beating, gradually fold in sifted flour until it is fully incorporated, about 2 minutes. Add anise oil and beat 1 minute. Mixture should be the texture of heavy whipped cream and hold to a wooden spoon.

2. Use a teaspoon to drop the cookies onto the greased cookie sheets, spreading at least 1 inch apart. Top each cookie with a pinch of nonpareil sprinkles. Allow cookies to sit in a cool, dry place several hours or overnight.

3. When ready to bake, preheat oven to 350°F. Bake until cookies have puffed and the bottoms are slightly browned, 15 minutes. Allow cookies to cool, then carefully remove from pan. Cool thoroughly before packaging. Anise cookies can be stored up to one week in an airtight container kept in a cool, dry place.

CUCCIDATI
(FIG COOKIES)

Makes 6 dozen

SPECIAL EQUIPMENT: *electric or hand-cranked food grinder*

No Sicilian holiday celebration would be complete without *cuccidati*. This recipe is for the bite-sized cookies. For recipe and directions for cutting the large decorative *cuccidati*, see page 123. For information on purchasing imported dried figs, see page 15. Although homegrown figs are delicious, their texture is not suitable for making this fig filling.

Photo by Anthony "Chopper" Leone.

Fig Filling

3 pounds dried Greek or Turkish figs
6 tablespoons honey
2 tablespoons ground cinnamon
2 tablespoons orange zest
1 pinch black pepper

1. Remove stems from dried figs. Rinse figs in warm water to soften, and thoroughly drain.

2. In a large bowl, coat figs with honey. Add cinnamon, orange zest, and black pepper, and mix well.

3. Use an electric or hand-cranked food grinder, not a food processor, and grind fig mixture to a fine texture. Divide mixture in half, wrap each half in plastic, and seal in plastic bags. This filling will keep covered in the refrigerator up to 6 weeks, or it can be frozen up to 6 months.

Cuccidati Dough

5 cups all-purpose flour
¾ cup white vegetable shortening
1½–2 cups warm water
¾ cup granulated sugar

1. In a large bowl, add flour and shortening and blend it with your fingers until it's the texture of cornmeal. Set aside.

2. In a separate bowl, add 1 cup warm water to sugar and mix completely to dissolve. Slowly add sugar water to flour mixture, blending until dough forms a ball. If dough is too dry, gradually add more water ¼ cup at a time. Cover dough with a damp towel and set aside 10 minutes.

3. Separate dough into 2 balls and knead each until smooth, about 3 minutes. Return dough balls to bowl and cover.

Cuccidati Icing

(Make after *cuccidati* are completely cooled.)

2 tablespoons milk or cream
2 drops almond extract
2 cups powdered sugar

Combine milk and almond extract. Gradually blend into sugar, and mix to a smooth paste. Icing should be the texture of heavy cream.

Cuccidati Assembly

Fig Filling
Cuccidati Dough
Cuccidati Icing
Colored nonpareils

1. Preheat oven to 300°F. Divide fig filling into 6 equal portions and shape each into 1×12-inch rolls. Cover with plastic wrap and set aside.

2. Working with one dough ball at a time, on a lightly floured surface, roll out a 12-inch square. It should be ⅛ inch thick. Cut the dough square into three 4×12-inch-long strips. Lay the rolls of filling vertically down the centers of each pastry strip. Carefully fold the side edges over to meet in the center and slightly overlap. Turn the filled pastry bar over, seam side down, and pat lightly to seal the edges and flatten.

3. Cutting on a 45-degree angle, slice each filled pastry bar into 1-inch-long *cuccidati.* Place them seam-side down 2 inches apart on an ungreased baking sheet. Put the pans in the oven. When fully baked, the bottoms will be slightly browned, but the tops should remain white. This takes 20–25 minutes. Thoroughly cool on a baking rack before icing.

4. When ready to ice, work over a small bowl and spoon icing over each cooled *cuccidata,* allowing excess to drip into the bowl. Dry iced *cuccidati* slightly before sprinkling with nonpareils. Allow *cuccidati* icing to dry thoroughly before packaging. They can be stored in sealed tins in a cool, dry place up to 1 week.

LEMON "S" COOKIES

Makes 5 dozen

Lemon "S" Cookies were the specialty of my maternal grandmother's dear friend Mary Guzzardi Cammarata. They are the perfect sweet bite to serve with a cup of espresso.

3½ cups all-purpose flour
3½ teaspoons baking powder
3½ tablespoons granulated sugar
3½ tablespoons lard or white vegetable shortening, room temperature
1 large egg
¾ cup milk
⅓ cup freshly squeezed lemon juice
1-pound box powdered sugar
Grated zest of 1 lemon

1. Preheat oven to 350°F. In a large bowl, sift together flour and baking powder. In a separate bowl, cream together sugar and shortening. (This takes about 5 minutes on medium mixer speed.) Lightly whisk egg and fold into sugar mixture. Make a well in the flour mixture, add in egg mixture, and mix lightly until fully incorporated. Stir in milk to form a soft dough. Cover and set aside 10 minutes.

2. Separate dough into 3 equal parts. Knead each to a smooth ball, about 1 minute, and return to bowl and cover. Break off small pieces of dough, about 2 tablespoons at a time, and roll each into a 12×½-inch-thick pencil-like strip. Cutting on a 45-degree angle, slice each strip into three 4-inch-long pieces. For each horizontal 4-inch piece, curl the left end up and the right end down to form an "S" shape. Place 1 inch apart on an ungreased baking sheet and pat each cookie to slightly flatten. Bake until bottoms of cookies are lightly browned, about 20 minutes. Thoroughly cool cookies before coating with icing.

3. When ready to ice, add lemon juice to powdered sugar and stir lightly until the mixture is smooth and the texture of light cream. Place ½ of the cooled cookies into a large bowl and pour icing over them. Mix lightly with a spatula or wooden spoon to thoroughly coat each cookie.

4. With a slotted spoon, carefully place cookies onto drying racks, spacing apart to avoid overcrowding. Repeat procedure with remaining cookies. Sprinkle lemon zest over cookies and allow to dry completely before packaging. Cookies can be kept in sealed containers stored in a cool place up to 1 week, or they can be frozen up to 3 weeks.

Photo by Cynthia LeJeune Nobles.

SCARDELLINI
(BRITTLE-TEXTURED WHITE COOKIES, ALSO KNOWN AS SKIDELINA AND OSSI DEI MORTI, BONES OF THE DEAD)

Makes 3 dozen (Begin 12–24 hours ahead.)

This recipe is adapted from *The New Orleans Italian Cookbook,* published in 1979 by the Italian American Society of Jefferson Auxiliary. The recipe contributor was Genevieve Harris, who had been an active member of the American-Italian community in Louisiana. *Scardellini* are crispy and resemble dried bone. They are usually prepared for All Soul's Day, celebrated on the second day of November in commemoration of all the faithful departed. They are also among the many Sicilian sweets found on St. Joseph Altars.

2 cups granulated sugar
1 cup all-purpose flour
1 teaspoon ground cinnamon
1 teaspoon allspice
¼ teaspoon baking powder
¼ teaspoon ground cloves
Zest of 1 orange
¼ cup water

1. In a large bowl, combine sugar, flour, cinnamon, allspice, baking powder, cloves, and orange zest. Add water and stir to form a stiff dough. Roll 4 tablespoons of dough at a time into 1×12-inch pencil-like logs. Cut the logs into 1½-inch pieces. Place pieces 1 inch apart on a parchment-paper-lined baking sheet and flatten slightly. Cover with a dry cloth and set aside 12–24 hours.

2. When ready to bake, heat your oven to 350°F. Uncover cookies and bake 12 minutes. Remove cookies promptly. If left in the oven too long, they will turn brown; they should remain white. Carefully remove cookies from parchment paper and place on baking racks to cool. As they cool, they will become crisp. *Scardellini* can be kept in airtight tins stored in a dry place at room temperature up to 1 week.

SESAME SEED COOKIES

Makes 10 dozen

Everyone seems to favor Sicilian sesame seed cookies, also called *biscotti regina,* which literally means "queen of biscuits" or "queen of cookies." They are crispy and only slightly sweet, and are the perfect accompaniment to an afternoon cup of cappuccino.

2 cups unhulled sesame seeds
1¾ cups granulated sugar, divided
4¼ cups all-purpose flour
1 teaspoon baking powder
½ teaspoon salt
2 large eggs
1 cup white vegetable shortening
½ cup milk
2 tablespoons pure vanilla extract

1. Preheat oven to 350°F. In a fine mesh strainer, rinse seeds under a thin stream of water. Drain seeds thoroughly and spread onto a baking sheet. Sprinkle with ¼ cup sugar. Stir and spread the seeds evenly on the baking sheet and place in the preheated oven. Bake 5 minutes and set aside.

Photo by Anthony "Chopper" Leone.

2. In a large bowl, sift together 4 cups flour, baking powder, and salt. Set aside. In a separate bowl, beat eggs with a mixer until foamy and gradually add remaining 1½ cups sugar. Add the shortening and mix until fully incorporated.

3. Make a well in the center of the flour mixture and fold in the egg mixture. Mix in the milk and vanilla. The dough should be workable but slightly sticky. If dough seems too sticky to knead, gradually add 1 tablespoon of flour at a time until you reach the desired consistency. Knead the dough a few minutes, separate it into 4 balls, and return the balls to the bowl. Cover and set aside 10 minutes.

4. Spread half the warm seeds in a 12-inch line on a dry, clean pastry board. Pinch off ½-cup pieces of dough and roll them into logs approximately ¾ inch thick. Roll each dough strip in the seeds, coating thoroughly on all sides. Cutting on a 45-degree angle, slice strips into 2-inch-long pieces. Place cookies on an ungreased baking sheet, spacing 1-inch apart. Repeat process with remaining dough and seeds until all are used. Pat each to slightly flatten and bake until brown on the bottom and slightly browned on top, about 20 minutes.

5. Cool cookies thoroughly before storing. Sesame seed cookies can be stored in sealed tins and kept in a cool place for 2 weeks, or they can be frozen up to 2 months.

COCONUT PRALINES

Makes 3 dozen

In the early days of New Orleans, these luscious candies were sold by street vendors, and they were particular favorites on Mardi Gras Day. Though not traditionally Sicilian, this confection is often found on Louisiana's St. Joseph Altars.

3 cups granulated sugar
1 cup whole milk
2 (3½-ounce) cans sweetened coconut
1 tablespoon butter
1 teaspoon vanilla extract
2 drops red food coloring

1. In a heavy-bottomed saucepan, combine sugar and milk. Bring to a full boil over high heat. Cook until liquid reduces to a syrup, about 3 minutes.

2. Reduce heat to medium and stir in coconut. Cook, stirring constantly with a wooden spoon, until mixture reaches the soft ball stage, 235°F, when a bit of hot mixture is dropped into a cup of iced water and can be rolled between your fingers into a soft ball.

3. Remove from heat. Add butter, vanilla, and red food coloring. Beat with a wooden spoon until mixture thickens and coats the spoon.

4. Quickly drop by tablespoonfuls onto a marble slab or wax paper, spacing 1 inch apart. Allow pralines to cool thoroughly. Carefully scrape pralines from marble slab. Individual pralines can be wrapped in wax paper and stored in a cool, dry place up to 2 weeks.

PECAN PRALINES

Makes 24 large or 36 petite pralines

- 2 cups light brown sugar, firmly packed
- 1 cup granulated sugar
- ½ cup, plus 2 tablespoons water
- 2 cups pecan halves
- 1 pinch salt
- 2 tablespoons butter
- 1 teaspoon pure vanilla extract or rum

1. In a heavy-bottomed saucepan, combine sugars. Stir in water and cook over high heat until mixture dissolves and reaches the boiling stage.

2. Add pecan halves and salt. Reduce heat to medium. Continue cooking, stirring with a wooden spoon, until syrup reached the soft ball stage, 235°F, when a drop of the hot syrup dropped into a cup of cold water can be rolled between your fingers into a soft ball. Remove from heat. Add butter and vanilla. Beat with a wooden spoon until mixture thickens and coats the spoon.

3. Drop by spoonsful onto a marble slab or wax paper, spacing about 1 inch apart. (One tablespoon makes a 2-inch praline, and 1 teaspoon makes a 1-inch or petite praline.) Allow pralines to cool thoroughly. Carefully scrape pralines from marble slab. Individual pralines can be wrapped in wax paper and stored in a cool, dry place up to 2 weeks.

TORRONE SICILIANO DI PINA
(SICILIAN ALMOND BRITTLE)

Makes 1 pound candy

This is a recipe from Maria Bertucci Compagno, retired owner of the former Campagno's Restaurant, now Vincent's Restaurant on St. Charles Avenue in New Orleans. Maria's Torrone Siciliano di Pina won first prize in a dessert competition held by the American Society of Italian Heritage. This recipe is from her cookbook, *Maria Bertucci Compagno's Sicilian-Style Cooking, From Ustica to New Orleans.* As stated by Maria, "My friend, Pina, makes this when I go to Ustica. This is one of her special Sicilian desserts, and also one of my favorites."

1 pound almonds, whole with skins on
2 cups granulated sugar
Zest of 1 lemon
1 tablespoon pure vanilla extract
½ teaspoon ground cinnamon
1 teaspoon vegetable oil

1. In a large skillet set over low heat, combine almonds and sugar. Stir constantly with a wooden spoon until sugar is dissolved. Stir in lemon zest, vanilla, and cinnamon. Cook until almonds are fully coated and sugar turns the color of maple syrup, about 4 minutes. (Don't overcook. As sugar darkens, the flavor becomes increasingly bitter.)

2. Pour mixture directly onto a marble slab or parchment paper. If using parchment paper, dampen the bottom to adhere to your work surface and lightly brush the top with ½ teaspoon vegetable oil.

3. Brush a sheet of parchment paper with ½ teaspoon vegetable oil and place the oiled side of the paper on top of the candy. Use a large, flat metal or wooden spatula to flatten mixture to an even ¾-inch thickness. When completely cooled, cut or break into pieces. Cooled torrone should be kept in a dry, cool place. Candy can be stored up to 1 week in airtight tins, using wax or parchment paper to separate layers.

POUND CAKE

Makes 8 servings

This family-favorite recipe is from my mother's sister, Lena Accardo Miller. Aunt Lena was known as a perfectionist who refused to use an electric mixer for her cake baking, preferring instead to "count the beats." I used an electric mixer to test this adaptation of her recipe.

1 tablespoon vegetable shortening
2 cups plus 1 tablespoon all-purpose flour
2 teaspoons baking powder
1 pinch salt
½ pound (2 sticks) salted butter, room temperature
1¾ cups granulated sugar
5 large eggs
1 tablespoon pure vanilla extract
FOR SERVING: ½ cup powdered sugar

1. Preheat oven to 350°F. Thoroughly grease the inside of a Bundt pan with vegetable shortening. Dust with 1 tablespoon flour and shake to loosen excess. Set aside.

2. Sift the 2 cups flour twice. Add baking powder and salt to flour and sift again. Set aside.

3. Using an electric mixer set at medium speed, cream together butter and sugar until mixture is light and fluffy, about 5 minutes. Add eggs, one at a time, beating after each addition. Reduce mixer speed to low. Gradually add in flour mixture and mix until fully incorporated, about 2 minutes. Stir in vanilla. Pour batter into prepared Bundt pan.

4. Bake until cake springs back when lightly pressed on top, about 50 minutes. Allow cake to cool thoroughly before removing from pan. To serve, dust with powdered sugar.

STRAWBERRY CREAM CAKE

Makes 8–10 servings

My paternal great-grandparents, Giorgio and Virginia Maturana, were strawberry farmers in Tangipahoa Parish, Louisiana. When fresh strawberries are at their springtime prime, this luscious homemade cake with sweetened whipped cream is among our family's favorite desserts.

Cake

1 tablespoon vegetable shortening
¾ cup all-purpose flour, plus more for dusting pans
6 large eggs, room temperature, separated
¾ cup granulated sugar
1 tablespoon vanilla
¼ teaspoon cornstarch
1 pinch salt
1 teaspoon oil of anise

1. Preheat oven to 350°F. Coat three 9-inch cake pans with vegetable shortening and lightly dust with flour. Remove excess flour and set the pans aside.

2. In a medium bowl, beat egg whites to a stiff peak. Set aside. In a large bowl, add sugar, then egg yolks, and beat until doubled in volume, about 5 minutes. Add vanilla and set aside.

3. In a separate bowl, sift together ¾ cup flour, cornstarch, and salt. Fold dry ingredients into egg yolk mixture. Stir in anise oil. Gently fold in beaten egg whites.

4. Divide batter evenly among prepared cake pans. Bake until layers are slightly browned and tops are springy to the touch, 40–50 minutes. Remove from oven and cool on wire racks. When thoroughly cooled, carefully remove cakes from pans and set aside.

Cream Filling

1 quart heavy cream
4 tablespoons granulated sugar
2 drops oil of anise

Whip cream until slightly stiff. Continue whipping and gradually add sugar until fully incorporated. Stir in anise oil. Refrigerate until needed.

Cake Assembly

2 pints fresh strawberries, hulled and sliced, reserving 6 large strawberries with stems
3 tablespoons granulated sugar
3 tablespoons maraschino liqueur, divided
Cake layers
Cream Filling

1. Place strawberries in a large bowl and stir in sugar. Toss lightly with 1 tablespoon Maraschino liqueur and refrigerate. Lightly sprinkle the tops of the cooled cake layers with the remaining 2 tablespoons maraschino liqueur.

2. Place one cake layer on a serving plate and top it evenly with half of the sugared strawberries, then 1 cup whipped cream. Top with another cake layer and repeat the process. Top with the third cake layer and cover top and sides of cake with remaining whipped cream.

3. Refrigerate at least one hour to allow flavors to set. Before serving, slice the remaining 6 strawberries in half and use them to garnish the bottom edge of the cake. Serve immediately.

CUCCIA DI SANTA LUCIA
(ST. LUCIA'S HONEY-SWEETENED WHEAT CUSTARD)

Makes 6 servings (begin the day ahead)

Cuccia is the traditional wheat custard served to commemorate the Feast of Santa Lucia, December 13. Legend tells of the arrival in Sicily of a shipment of wheat on Lucia's feast day, which provided sustenance during a famine. Still following the tradition established centuries ago, many families of Sicilian heritage serve *cuccia* on the Feast of St. Lucy, but they will eat no bread.

1 cup whole uncooked wheat berries
Water
¾ cup honey, divided
¼ teaspoon salt
Grated zest of 1 lemon

1. In a bowl, soak wheat berries in cold water and refrigerate overnight. Strain and rinse wheat berries in cold running water. Strain again.

2. In a heavy-bottomed saucepan set over medium heat, add soaked wheat berries. Add 2 cups water and bring to a full boil. Reduce heat to a simmer. Add ½ cup honey and salt. Cook, stirring occasionally, until kernels burst open, approximately 1 hour. Add ½ cup water if needed to avoid sticking. The cooked wheat should be creamy, but still slightly chewy.

3. Spoon custard into individual serving bowls. Warm remaining ¼ cup honey, drizzle over each serving. Top with a pinch of grated lemon zest and serve.

FRESH RICOTTA
(RECOOKED MILK)

Makes 1 quart

A friend whose family had been dairy farmers for generations gave this recipe to my mother. Because fresh ricotta has no salt, it is preferred in sweet desserts such as *cassateda* or cannoli. When you're finished straining the milk curds, you'll end up with a bowl of whey. For lagniappe, you can make a spectacular soup with the whey by bringing it to a boil and adding broccoli or any type of fresh greens. Then add pasta and finish with Parmesan cheese, extra virgin olive oil, and fresh basil.

SPECIAL EQUIPMENT: *cheesecloth*

1 gallon whole milk

1 quart buttermilk

1. Line a colander or strainer with cheesecloth and set it over a large bowl. In a large pot set over medium heat, slowly heat the whole milk, just until tiny bubbles appear along the rim of the pot. Reduce heat to a simmer.

2. In a separate pot, slowly warm the buttermilk until small bubbles appear along the rim, at approximately 200°F. Slowly stream the warm buttermilk into the whole milk, stirring the whole while. Curds should start appearing.

3. With a slotted spoon, scoop curds out of the simmering pot and into the prepared colander. As milk continues to simmer and curds rise to the top, remove them and strain through the cheesecloth. Continue until all curds are removed.

4. Twist the cheesecloth to strain out excess liquid. Reserve the whey for another use. Remove ricotta to a clean bowl and cover with plastic wrap. Refrigerate immediately. Since fresh ricotta has no preservatives, it is very delicate and should be consumed within 2 days. Fresh ricotta can also be frozen up to 3 weeks.

LIMONCELLO
(LEMON LIQUEUR)

Makes 2½ fifths

This recipe is listed as the "House Specialty" in *Maria Bertucci Compagno's Sicilian-Style Cooking, From Ustica to New Orleans.* As stated by Maria, "Limoncello was a gift from my friend, Emilia Salerno, brought from Ustica by Pietro (Maria's cousin). On one of my trips to Ustica, I obtained the recipe and have made it ever since. Everyone loves it!" Maria suggests picking the lemons before they are fully ripe, while they are still mostly green and just turning yellow.

6–8 large lemons, preferably homegrown
1 liter Everclear grain alcohol
1½ liters (6⅓ cups) water
3 cups granulated sugar

1. If using homegrown lemons, rinse and dry them. If using commercially produced lemons, scrub skins to remove pesticide residue and waxy coating and dry them. Use a potato peeler to peel off lemon rinds, and reserve. Avoid cutting into the white pith. Save peeled lemons for another use.

2. Place lemon peels into a glass gallon jar. Add Everclear and cap the jar. Every day for 1 week, stir gently to mix.

3. After 7 days, add water and sugar to a pot, bring to a full boil, and cook 4 minutes. Remove from fire and cool completely.

4. Add the Everclear and lemon peel and mix well. Set aside 20 minutes, then strain. Funnel limoncello into sterilized bottles and seal with screw tops or corks. Store bottles upright in a cool, dark place at least 3 weeks to allow flavors to fully develop. Store matured, sealed bottles in a freezer. Limoncello is best served cold as an after-dinner *digestivo,* a digestive cordial.

8

Display *Cuccidati* and Designs

The Italian fig cookies known as *cuccidati* come in all sizes. Prominently displayed on many St. Joseph Altars are the large, elaborately designed *cuccidati* also regionally known as *spada*. These *cuccidati* are made with basically the same recipe used for the smaller fig cookie that goes by the same name, with the exception of the use of a stiffer dough that better holds up the larger pastry's lacy designs.

Photo by Anthony "Chopper" Leone.

Cuccidati displayed on a St. Joseph Altar at St. Mary's Dominican High School, New Orleans.

Each individual design is made of a pastry dough base covered with a layer of fig paste and then overlaid with another layer of pastry intricately hand-carved into a lacy pattern. Some display *cuccidati* can be as large as twenty-eight inches wide, while others, such as the Santa Lucia plate and the plate of St. Joseph, can be as small as twelve inches across. I have always been fascinated by the rich designs carved into these pastries, and of the meanings those designs represent.

These works of art are a continuity of centuries-old tradition, and individual designs are often passed down from generation to generation. Each of these icons depicts a specific religious symbol, and each symbol tells the story of the figure it represents. As a child in New Orleans during the 1940s, I could recognize distinctive designs, identifying which family had prepared a *cuccidata* by the nuances of their carving techniques.

The many years I spent in the kitchen with my grandmother Accardo preparing *cuccidati* for her St. Joseph Altars were sacred experiences. Her work surfaces were organized with gleaming bowls for mixing pastry and trays of fig paste arranged in neat rolls. I was mesmerized by her assemblage of simple culinary tools. Some of her handmade carving tools were brought with her from Sicily. I watched in awe as her hands seemed to fly as she rolled out dough, pressed in fig paste, and overlaid the top pastry sheet, creating a totally original design, all without the aid of a picture or a tracing to guide her. What lives within me still is the memory of her simple, whispered prayer, repeated with each cut of the three-leafed *cuccidata* edging—Gesù, Maria, Giuseppe.

Just as stained-glass windows of medieval cathedrals served to interpret Holy Scripture in the Middle Ages, *cuccidati* designs today bring to life the stories of their sacred symbols. In my family, the variety of symbolic *cuccidati* typically includes the cross, designed with flowers in bloom to symbolize the Risen Christ, the Sacred Heart of Mary, designed with a flame to symbolize Mary's faith, and the staff of St. Joseph, a representation of the legend of St. Joseph's simple walking stick, which sprouts a lily, the symbol of St. Joseph's purity.

Other notable *cuccidati* designs include the monstrance or ostensorium, a representation of the vessel that holds the Eucharist, and the ancient Arbëreshë symbol of the double-headed eagle, a representation of unity between church and state and of the Eastern and Western Churches. My maternal grand-

Sacred Heart of Mary design.
Photo by Anthony "Chopper" Leone.

mother's sister, Rosalie Caronna Canal, taught me that the interior design of flowers and branches connected to a singular stem represents unity with Christ. Individual flowers carved with three petals represent the Holy Family, and with five petals they symbolize the five sacred wounds of Christ.

When I moved to Mandeville in the early 1980s, I connected with a cousin of my grandmother, Sister Gerome Roppolo of the Order of St. Benedict, who was teaching at Our Lady of the Lake School in Mandeville, and who lived at St. Scholastica Priory in Covington, Louisiana. It was Sister Gerome who provided definitive answers about the religious symbolism of display *cuccidati*. Sister Gerome also taught me the techniques of quilling, shaping, and cutting dough. She explained that the ancient art of paper quilling, applied to specific *cuccidati* designs, has many meanings, such as a representation of the flame of the Sacred Heart of Mary, or the blooming of the lily of St. Joseph's staff.

Over the years I have been fortunate to make several trips to Poggioreale, Italy, the ancestral home of my maternal grandmother. Aside from flying off on fantastic vacations, I went to this small agricultural town in the province of Trapani to learn about *cuccidati* designs from family members still living there. One particularly memorable trip was in 2007, when I spent time baking with Poggioreale members of l'Associazione Pro Loco, the Pro Loco Association, a nationwide network of volunteers who work to preserve Italian culture. The exquisite *cuccidati* artistry of Pro Loco Association members resembles lace and is called *squartucciati,* which means lace making. Working in their kitchen was like stepping back in time to my grandmother's kitchen. Their assemblage of ingredients, tools, and even the neat rolls of fig paste were exactly as I recall from my grandmother. Most reassuring were their recipes, which were the same as those my grandmother handed down to our family.

I now use my grandmother's simple *cuccidata* carving tools, and each time I pick one up I know she is still there beside me, guiding my hands in continuing this sacred tradition. I also use those tools when I teach about *cuccidati* making. And even though I have many passionate students, as the years go on, I feel that the practice of creating *cuccidati* might be at risk of becoming a lost art. My fears especially grow each time I hear that for some St. Joseph Altars

Carving tools. Photo by Cynthia LeJeune Nobles.

Monstrance design.
Photo by Anthony "Chopper" Leone.

the *cuccidati* are prepared with nonedible dough, or they are packaged and frozen to be displayed again year after year. "Convenience" *cuccidati* certainly make things easier, but these large cookies, though spectacularly beautiful, are meant to be eaten. In the tradition of offering the finest of culinary artistry to honor St. Joseph, these elaborate pastry designs are supposed to be part of the shared feast.

Symbolism of Traditional Cuccidati *Designs*

Basket	*Abbondanza* (abundance of blessings)
Chalice	Consecration of Christ
Circle	Eternal love

Symbol	Meaning
Cross	Risen Christ Faith
Double-headed eagle	Byzantine symbol representing God and country, heaven and earth, the Eastern and Western Churches Faith
Dove	Peace
Eyes of St. Lucy plate	Light of faith Martyrdom of Santa Lucia
Fish	Early Christian symbol Faith
Heart	Sacred Heart of Mary Love
Monstrance or ostensorium	Vessel that holds the Sacred Host venerated at Benediction Body of Christ
Palm	Victory Eternal life Peace
Peacock	Ancient symbol of rebirth Hope
Sandals	Walking in the footsteps of Christ Humility
Staff	St. Joseph's walking stick sprouting a lily Purity
Rosary	Prayer to the Blessed Mother Faith

DISPLAY CUCCIDATI
(EDIBLE DISPLAY FIG COOKIES)

Makes three 18-inch fig-filled pastries

Traditionally, decorative *cuccidati* are prominently stood upright on St. Joseph Altars so the designs can easily be seen. The following recipe for *cuccidati* is for an edible stiff dough that will support the designs for display. For additional support, cut a heavy foam board in the shape of your *cuccidata* and secure it behind the pastry with a simple powdered-sugar and water paste.

Since these elaborate designs of fig-filled pastry are prepared with love, they are generously shared and are meant to be eaten, usually with family and friends at a celebratory meal.

Fig Paste Filling

Makes enough for three 18-inch cuccidati

SPECIAL EQUIPMENT: *electric or hand-cranked food grinder*

10 pounds dried Greek or Turkish figs
¼ cup honey
7 tablespoons cinnamon
½ cup grated orange zest
¾ teaspoon ground black pepper

1. Remove stems from dried figs. Rinse figs in warm water to soften, and thoroughly drain them. In a large bowl, coat figs with honey and stir in cinnamon. Add orange zest and black pepper, and mix well.

2. Use an electric or hand-cranked food grinder, not a food processor, to finely grind the fig mixture. Divide mixture into 1-pound packages, wrap each in plastic, and seal in plastic food-storage bags. Fig Paste Filling will keep covered in the refrigerator up to 6 weeks, or it can be frozen up to 6 months.

Cuccidati Dough

Makes three 18-inch cuccidati

5 pounds all-purpose flour
2 cups white vegetable shortening
3–4 cups warm water
2 cups granulated sugar

1. In the bowl of a standing electric mixer fitted with a paddle attachment, add flour, then shortening, and blend over low speed until the texture of cornmeal. Set aside.

2. In a separate bowl, combine 3 cups warm water and sugar and stir until dissolved. Using medium mixer speed, gradually add sugar mixture into flour mixture. Mix until dough forms a stiff ball. If it's too dry, gradually add more water ¼ cup at a time. Knead to form a smooth ball, about 3 minutes. Cover and set it aside 10 minutes.

3. Separate dough into 3 balls. Each should be about 6 inches across. Knead each ball until smooth, about 5 minutes, and return them to the bowl. Cover and set aside for 10 minutes.

Cuccidati Assembly

SPECIAL EQUIPMENT: *six to eight 9¾-inch-long wood skewers*

1. Preheat oven to 200°F. Decide the shape of *cuccidata* you want to make, and on a clean sheet of parchment paper, trace your design with a pencil. This shape determines the size and basic shape of the pastry sheet you will roll out. (Working with a 20×20-inch sheet of rolled dough will be sufficient for most shapes.)

2. Use 1 dough ball for each *cuccidata*. Separate a dough ball in half, and cover and set aside the half you are not working on. On a hard, floured surface, roll the half ball of dough to a 20-inch square that's ⅓-inch thick. Transfer rolled-out pastry onto a sheet of parchment paper. Place the clean side of the traced paper directly over the rolled-out dough, with the pencil tracing facing

up. Transfer the design onto the dough by lightly tracing the outline with a small knife, pressing an impression onto the dough without cutting into the dough. Remove and discard parchment paper with the pencil tracing.

3. Spread a ¼-inch-thick layer of fig paste inside the dough-design impression, leaving a 1-inch border of plain dough. To stabilize the *cuccidata,* press 2 or 3 wood skewers into the fig paste where needed. (Each *cuccidata* design will dictate placement of skewers. Smaller designs do not require skewers.) Trim the skewers to the size of the *cuccidati* before you place them onto the fig paste. Cover skewers with additional fig paste. Use your fingertips to press on the fig paste to conceal the skewers. Cover with a fresh piece of parchment paper or a clean dry cloth and set aside.

4. Roll out the remaining dough ball half to an approximate 20-inch square that's ⅓ inch thick. Carefully fit the second pastry sheet over the fig-filled design. Carefully trace along the outside edges of the fig-filled design with your fingertips, pressing down to seal the dough together and leaving a 1-inch border. Use a decorative cutting tool to cut off excess edges of dough and to create a design along the entire 1-inch border.

5. Use a small sharp knife to create designs in the dough. If you want to make flowers, cut through the top layer of dough into the filling and design several flowers with their petals, leaves, and stems. When you are finished cutting your basic flowers, make cuts that attach the flowers and stems to one singular stem. To reveal the cut work, through the top layer of dough and into the fig filling, make a continuous cut ½ inch from the *cuccidata*'s outside border. Cut all the way around the interior of the design. Carefully peel away excess dough from the cut design, revealing the cut flowers and stems that will remain over the fig filling. Set aside excess dough for future use. To finish the design, use a wooden skewer or a pecan pick to press tiny indentions into the center of the flower petals. Smooth out any ragged pastry edges and refine your design by pressing small indentations into flower petals and leaves.

6. Transfer the *cuccidata* on its parchment paper onto a large baking sheet. Bake until *cuccidata* is fully dried, at least 1 hour. A fully baked *cuccidata* will be a matte-white color, not brown. When removed from the oven, if the dough

has a spotty look, continue baking an additional ½ hour. Some large *cuccidata* designs require 2 hours of baking time. Allow *cuccidata* to cool completely, at least 8 hours or overnight.

7. Each *cuccidata* can be covered in shrink-wrap, which is usually available at hobby specialty stores the weeks before Easter. Baked *cuccidati* can be stored in a cool dry place up to 1 week. If securely wrapped, they can be frozen up to 1 month. Unbaked *cuccidati* can be frozen up to 2 weeks. Before baking frozen *cuccidati,* fully defrost, which will take at least overnight in a cool dry place (not in a refrigerator, which can add moisture). Follow directions for baking fresh *cuccidata*.

9

Symbolism of Foods and Elements

Many symbolic foods displayed on St. Joseph Altars are repetitions of the *cuccidati* designs listed in chapter 8. The following is a listing of additional foods and other elements traditionally found on St. Joseph Altars.

Specialty breads (fish and cross), cakes, and *pignolati* on display.

BISCOTTI

Pignolati (pinecone-shaped mounds of fried dough balls)	The simple toys of the Child Jesus Humility
Pupa cu l'ova (pastry over egg formed into shapes of baby chicks)	The rebirth of spring Hope
Scardallini (confection also known as *ossi dei morti*)	Bones of the Dead Mortality

BREADS

Circle	Everlasting love
Cross	Crucifixion of Christ
Fish	Early Christian symbol of Christ
Heart	Love of the Blessed Virgin Mary
Palm	Victory Eternal life Peace
Ladder (from biblical account of Jacob's dream)	Union of heaven and earth Faith
Mudica	Representation of sawdust in St. Joseph's workshop Humility

CAKES

Bible	Word of God
Candles	Symbols of promise, petition, thanksgiving, remembrance
Lamb	Sacrificial Lamb of God Love, sacrifice

FISH

Baked redfish	Bounty from the sea Early Christian symbol
Seven fish	Seven Sacraments
Twelve fish	Twelve apostles

FLOWERS AND PLANTS

Ferns	Humility Crown of thorns
Fig leaves	Fertility
Lemon sprigs	Fidelity of love
Lilies	Purity
Olive branch	Peace
Orange blossoms	Purity, chastity, generosity
Palms	Christian martyrdom Victory over death
Roses	Mary, the Blessed Mother

FRUIT

Almond	Blessed Virgin and resurrection of Christ
Apples	Eternal salvation
Cherries	Sweetness of salvation
Chestnut	Chastity
Figs	Fertility Faith
Grapes	Blood of Christ
Lemons	Fidelity

Oranges	Purity
Peach	Truth
Pineapple	Hospitality
Pomegranates	Fertility Resurrection of Christ
Strawberries	Harmony

VEGETABLES

Artichokes	Peace Prosperity
Cecida (Chickpeas)	Occhi di Santa Lucia (Eyes of St. Lucy) Sacrifice
Fava bean, or lucky bean	Abundance Resilience Hope
Olives	Peace
Wheat	Seasons of life Resurrection Faith

10

Abbondanza Blessings

There is a joyful provenance of devotional faith associated with the St. Joseph Altar tradition. This trust in Divine Providence has resulted in many family stories of small miracles, blessings received from participating in St. Joseph Altars. During St. Joseph's Feast days, as you visit with family, friends, and even perfect strangers, you too might be told these countless little miracles. Here are several that are testaments to homage and affection for St. Joseph.

Angelina's Prayers

On a cold winter's night in the early 1930s, with the whole family asleep, the house was finally still. In the early years of the twentieth century, Angelina Caronna had left Poggioreale for New Orleans, where she met and married Giuseppe Accardo. These were my maternal grandparents, and it was in New Orleans that they established their family and owned a grocery store. Now they had eight children, and the late-night quiet was Angelina's time for reflecting on the day's activities, for planning how the family would manage during the current worldwide economic depression, and for turning her thoughts to prayer.

Angelina felt particularly blessed, with her houseful of healthy children and a kind and gentle husband. She didn't mind putting in long days managing their store's business affairs, which included negotiating shelf-stock costs and setting retail prices. She also believed her contribution could not compare to Giuseppe's hardworking physical strength, which was the backbone of their business.

Threading her needle through linen, she continued praying and stitching her intricate embroidery designs. Her prayers turned back to thoughts. These past years had been particularly difficult financially in New Orleans, not only for the Accardos, but also for most of their neighboring immigrant families, many of whom lived beside their own corner grocery stores. They all shared the burden she now faced, of how to buy stock for their shelves while still managing to feed their families. Things were extremely challenging now that she and Giuseppe had just spent the last of their cash.

Angelina worried terribly about how they would manage, and she closed her eyes in prayer, "Gesù, Maria e San Giuseppe, help me to find a way." Her thoughts turned to the weeks ahead. She should be planning for the St. Joseph Altar, but didn't see how it was possible for this year. "Oh, San Giuseppe," she prayed aloud. "Ever since leaving Poggioreale we have honored your feast day with a St. Joseph Altar at our home in New Orleans. Please help me, so that I will not fail in our Promise."

Just then, Angelina heard a gentle knock at her door. She thought it was just the wind, but she looked up and saw a lady standing outside. She wondered who would be out on this cold, windy night, then recognized her caller. She opened the door to welcome a local seamstress, a daughter of her good friend Mrs. Cammarata, who announced she was there to pay for the embroidery work Angelina had done for weddings last June. The young woman handed Angelina a fifty-dollar bill.

Overwhelmed, Angelina held back tears and thanked her guest. As the woman left, Angelina sank to her knees to give thanks to San Giuseppe. With that money she bought sacks of flour, rice, and beans to sell, which quickly doubled her profit and gave her the opportunity to buy more stock. Normally, Angelina would have had her altar preparations ready early in the year. But in this midst of the Great Depression, she had not had enough set aside to buy supplies until mid-March. Word got out that my grandmother was preparing for an altar, and soon friends and business suppliers were calling and asking her to send someone by to pick up donations.

For the remainder of her life, Angelina never failed in her promise to San Giuseppe. Through the years, those donations continued to grow, from simple baskets of fruit to sacks of sugar or flour, to cases of eggs and bushels of vegetables. Each year during the weeks before March 19, family and friends would gather in her kitchen to prepare a feast to share with their community, welcoming guests to partake in each year's magnificent St. Joseph Altar celebration.

Prayers of Thanksgiving

In 1936, as Rosie Schiro Galioto was filling her mother's St. Joseph Altar with the last *cuccidati* and loaves of bread, she gave a silent prayer of thanks to St. Joseph. Five years earlier both her legs had been broken in a devastating automobile accident. On that fateful day, Rosie watched in horror as her young daughter, Mae Margaret, dashed into the street, right toward the path of an oncoming car. Though she was able to push the child away from the car's path, Rosie was caught under the car's wheels and spent the next two months in New Orleans's Charity Hospital.

Even when she was allowed to go home, the news from doctors was not good. Her bones had not healed properly, and there was no guarantee she would walk again. To facilitate proper healing, doctors suggested breaking her legs once more so her bones could be reset. Rosie's mother, Maria Pecoraro Schiro, who had grieved through the agonizing journey of her daughter's suffering, objected to this procedure. In prayers, she put Rosie into the hands of St. Joseph with a promise that on each following year their family would honor his feast day with a St. Joseph Altar.

Eventually, without breaking her bones again, Rosie walked with the help of crutches. Five years later, in 1936, on the week before St. Joseph's Day, Rosie Galioto stood and walked without any aid. The doctors confirmed she was completely healed and that her legs were stronger than before the accident.

The Schiro family fulfilled their promise and held an annual St. Joseph Altar in their home, which was beside their grocery store on Thalia Street in New Orleans. In the following years, Rosie Galioto's two daughters, Mae Margaret and Mary Ann, each had turns representing the Virgin Mary as a saint for their grandmother's St. Joseph Altar. Rosie and Mary Ann are deceased, but Mae still volunteers at local St. Joseph Altars.

Lucky Bean Sprouts

It was a breath of fresh air for the Sisters of the Good Shepherd when they moved to a new, sprawling campus on the banks of the Mississippi River in Bridge City. This modern home reflected its early 1960s architecture, especially with its bright open spaces. It was quite different from their dark New Orleans convent on the corner of Bienville and Broad streets, where their order had been housed over the past century. With room to grow, there was a plan for expansion as funds became available. High on the list of needed buildings was a full gymnasium equipped for volleyball and basketball tournaments, and with space for assemblies and a stage for performances.

Led by my grandmother Accardo, her group of volunteers had originally brought the tradition of the St. Joseph Altar to the Convent of the Good Shepherd in the mid-1940s, a time when an overflow of visitors had outgrown many of the altars in private homes. The displays at the Bienville Street convent had been open to the public for over twenty years, and thousands of visitors had

St. Joseph Altar at Convent of the Good Shepherd, New Orleans, ca. 1960.

participated in this sacred tradition. These visitors were also generous to the Sisters of the Good Shepherd, and their monetary donations had become a welcome addition to the convent's annual budget.

It was with great excitement that my grandmother and her volunteers prepared for that first St. Joseph Altar in Bridge City in 1962. And even though some wondered if visitors would make the pilgrimage "all the way to the Westbank," that inaugural altar at the nuns' new home saw more visitors than ever. Each year following, as more people heard about the huge St. Joseph Altar at the convent near the Mississippi River, steady streams of visitors filed through to witness the magnificent display. They would then progress to outdoor tables set up for serving the traditional Feast of St. Joseph, where countless plates of *pasta con le sarde* topped with *mudica* were served, along with tastes of fried *carduni, froscia,* and stuffed artichokes. By tradition, none of these blessed foods were allowed to be wasted. After feeding everyone, the St. Joseph Altar would be taken apart and the blessed foods, including breads, cooked foods, cakes, and confections were boxed for distribution to the community.

By St. Joseph's Day of 1966, the Bridge City St. Joseph Altar was a huge success, with record numbers of visitors annually viewing the display, and with the nuns' bank account continually growing. The morning following that year's event, my grandmother was gathering her table linens, punch bowls, and decorative dishes, and the kitchen manager asked her what she should do with the bowls of leftover lucky beans. The beans were blessed, and because they had been roasted, they could not be eaten. My grandmother replied that the beans should just be tossed into the yard for the birds. After the beans' hard, roasted outer shells had fallen off, the birds could eat them. The kitchen manager took my grandmother's suggestion.

During Holy Week that year, the kitchen manager noticed a patch of bright green in the nearby kitchen yard, and realized this was where she had tossed the lucky beans. She pointed out the patch of sprouts to the Mother Superior, who called my grandmother to announce, "Mrs. Accardo, we know where our new gymnasium will be built, it's where the Lucky Beans have sprouted! And thanks to St. Joseph, we now have the funds to begin construction."

The new gymnasium was completed in early 1968. By St. Joseph's Day of that year, it became the setting for the grandest St. Joseph Altar ever, and it was dedicated to the memory of Angelina Caronna Accardo, who took her last breath on December 16, 1967.

Heaven-Sent Helping Hands

It was on All Saints Day that, following a routine mammogram, I received a phone call cautioning that a closer look was needed, possibly a biopsy to determine if a suspicious mass was in fact cancerous. The biopsy was positive, and immediate surgery was suggested. I protested, because my husband and I already had plans for spending Christmas in Mexico.

The previous school year, my husband and I had hosted an exchange student from Campeche in our home, and we were planning to spend Christmas week visiting with his family. Even though it was already November and my surgeon insisted surgery could not wait, he also assured me that, after the operation, I would still be able to travel to Mexico by Christmas. What followed was a complete mastectomy of my right breast. On Thanksgiving Day, I was given the wonderful news that I was completely cancer free. On Christmas Day we were on the plane for a direct flight to the Yucatán, where we spent an amazing week of celebrating Feliz Navidad.

By early March, when preparations were already underway for the St. Joseph Altar at our parish church, St. Anselm's, I still had not recovered full strength in my right arm. I called our parish coordinator and explained that I was planning on coming to help. I also said that I could possibly carve the intricate *cuccidati* designs, but would not have the strength for rolling out the large layers of dough needed for making the *cuccidati* pastry. Her reply, which I had heard countless times from my maternal grandmother was, "Don't worry. St. Joseph always provides."

The following week, as we assembled supplies in the kitchen of St. Joseph's Hall, in walked a hefty-looking gentleman none of us recognized as a member of St. Anselm's Parish. Without even an introduction he told us he worked offshore, but this week he was on leave and decided he wanted to help with the St. Joseph Altar. "I don't know what I can do," he said, "but here I am."

We immediately set up a work station for him. With his powerful arms he eased through rolling out all of the dough, making it ready for carving into various *cuccidati* shapes. He later told us he had never before worked on a St. Joseph Altar but saw a newspaper article announcing plans for preparations at St. Anselm's and just came over to see how he could help.

The Three Lemons

Within the St. Joseph Altar tradition are many rituals and practices that vary from areas, communities, and families. Among the many beliefs is that St. Joseph intercedes for a variety of prayerful requests, from help in securing a job to selling a house. One unique practice is the belief that, if an unmarried woman takes a lemon from an altar, St. Joseph will assist in finding her a husband. This story is a case of going above and beyond expectations.

The St. Joseph Altar prepared by Anne and Michael Dale had gained a reputation for its creative display. St. Joseph's Day of 2011 was their sixth year hosting the altar in the showroom of their store, Anne Dale Jewelers, located on St. Ann Street in Mandeville, Louisiana. The cooperative effort of preparing the specialty foods and cookies for the altar was shared by Anne's family, the Ferraras, and their many friends, and Anne and Michael's discerning jeweler's eyes added an element of exquisite design to their project.

When Anne and Michael's friends Erin and Shelley Belk arrived to visit the altar, they mentioned to Michael that they'd been trying to have a family, but there was no baby yet. Michael reminded the couple that St. Joseph was known for helping find a husband, and he suggested that maybe he worked for babies too. He then handed Shelley three lemons. Shelley took the lemons home and slept with them tucked beneath her pillow. A few months later, Anne received a phone call from Erin, who told her Shelley was pregnant, with triplets. On November 10, 2012, three beautiful babies, Sadie, Toby and Tyler, were born. Triple blessings, thanks to St. Joseph.

11

A Labor of Love

As I look back on my many years of preparing St. Joseph Altars, I do so fondly, recalling the countless hours of building and dressing the altars and baking and cooking specialty foods. I am especially gratified that this tradition continues, and that it brings together communities of friends, family, and neighbors who, despite their arduous commitments of time, work happily together in honor of St. Joseph.

To me, helping build a St. Joseph Altar is best described as a labor of love, and participating in this ritual is more about the love than the labor. Over the years that love has come from both expected and unexpected places, as more and more communities show interest in St. Joseph Altars.

Foundations

As a child, when I first encountered St. Joseph Altar preparations in Mommie Accardo's kitchen, I tried to stay out of the way of her devoted crew of helpers. These helping hands included *cugini,* cousins who visited from out of state to assist with specialty baking. Our cousins would be joined by local Sicilian-born friends, who were members of la Società di Santa Lucia di New Orleans, the St. Lucy Society of New Orleans, which my grandmother had founded in 1927.

As the ladies rolled, cut, baked, and iced countless assorted cookies, I picked up snippets of their conversation, which was spoken in several Sicilian dialects, including ancient Arbëreshë, mixed with partial English. Though I couldn't quite understand all they said, I could tell by the exuberant tone of their words that their work in honor of San Giuseppe was truly a joyful experience.

I recall from my early years the elaborate St. Joseph Altars set up in the dining room of my grandparents' New Orleans home. In a true spirit of community, the altars were open to family, friends, and neighbors to share in the St. Joseph's Day feast. By the mid-1940s, the site of the altar was moved to the Convent of the Good Shepherd on Bienville Street in New Orleans. The more spacious setting of the convent's auditorium could accommodate the hundreds who came to see the display. But although the location had changed, annual preparations and specialty baking continued in my grandmother's kitchen in the weeks before March 19. Each year, I felt privileged to be there with Mommie Accardo's crew, to be enveloped by those amazing baking smells, and to learn the simple techniques of cutting small *cuccidati.*

In July of 1961, when the Sisters of the Good Shepherd closed their Bienville Street convent and moved to Bridge City, Louisiana, I continued helping

St. Joseph Altar at Convent of the Good Shepherd, New Orleans, 1961. Pictured are Madlyn Accardo Scalise, *left,* and Angelina Caronna Accardo.

with the nuns' St. Joseph Altar celebration by working in my grandmother's kitchen. Now a young adult, I would watch her carve the lacy designs of the large, decorative *cuccidati* and would ask if she could teach me. She always replied, "Next year; right now we are too busy." I contented myself by watching each special cut of her tiny knives and each different technique that embellished her designs. It was actually my grandmother's sisters who, in the late 1960s, taught me the technical *cuccidati* carving techniques. Sister Gerome Roppolo then taught me embellishment refinements in the 1980s, but the inspiration for my interest in the art came from my Mommie Accardo.

An Altar in City Park

St. Joseph Altar at Delgado Museum of Art, City Park, New Orleans, 1966. Giovanni Battista Tiepolo's painting *Saint Joseph and the Christ Child* appears above the altar. Photo by Stuart Lynn, courtesy of the author.

So prized were Mommie Accardo's *cuccidati* designs that in March 1966 an exhibit of her work went on display in a St. Joseph Altar at the Delgado Museum of Art in New Orleans's City Park. This venue represented a huge departure from the locations of the city's traditional St. Joseph Altars, before then displayed only in homes, in church communities, or in a few Sicilian-owned businesses.

Placed in a niche on the museum's ground floor, the three-tiered display featured specialty breads, *cuccidati,* and assorted biscotti. Above the altar was the magnificent painting *St. Joseph and the Christ Child* by the eighteenth-century Italian painter Giovanni Battista Tiepolo. The painting remains today as part of the permanent collection of the New Orleans Museum of Art.

A Display in New York

St. Joseph Altar on display at the Hallmark Gallery in New York, 1971.

In early 1970, a letter addressed to my grandmother Accardo arrived at her home. It was from the Hallmark Gallery in New York, requesting her assistance to produce a St. Joseph Altar that was to be part of the "Celebrations" exhibit being organized by food journalist Mimi Sheraton. When the letter arrived, we were all stunned with sadness since my grandmother had passed away in December of 1967.

But Mommie Accardo's death did not deter us. Even though one family member insisted it would be impossible to produce and ship a St. Joseph Altar all the way to New York, my mother and I were determined to make it happen. In mid-September, with a crew of helpers and my grandmother's sister, my great-aunt Rosalie Canal, we began our work.

Over the next few weeks, we produced enough decorative *cuccidati, pignolati,* assorted biscotti, and symbolic breads to fill a small St. Joseph Altar. Though this was the first time I had carved *cuccidati* designs, as I picked up my grandmother's simple tools, it was as though her hands were guiding me, and I successfully created the elaborate pastries.

We carefully packaged the baked goods into cartons. Hallmark sent three airline tickets, one for my mother, one for me, and one for the cartons of pastries. On September 28, we arrived in Manhattan, took a cab to the Hallmark Gallery on Fifth Avenue, and delivered the packages directly into the hands of Mimi Sheraton. Over the next two days, Ms. Sheraton's assistants decorated a St. Joseph Altar they had built to our specifications. To preserve the foods for the duration of the exhibit, the organizers coated each decorative piece with an acrylic spray.

By October 1, the gorgeous altar they had assembled was open to the public. Hundreds of visitors attended the exhibit each week, where it remained on display until January 7, 1971. Ms. Sheraton was delighted with the exhibit's success, particularly because of the interest from New Yorkers in the St. Joseph Altar tradition. While thanking us, she said that when she began planning the exhibit she did not realize that this Sicilian tradition was unique to Louisiana. When she first contacted her New York friends of Italian heritage, none had ever heard of a St. Joseph Altar. In those days before the Internet, how did she find us? A friend of hers, the New Orleans restaurateur William Guste of Antoine's Restaurant, had directed her to our family.

An Altar at the World's Fair

When plans for the 1984 Louisiana World's Fair were getting underway, I received an invitation from Joseph Maselli, chairman of the fair's Italian Village, to attend a planning meeting for a St. Joseph Altar exhibit that would be on display for the duration of the fair. In that meeting was Italian-born New Orleans artist Franco Alessandrini, who was to be the Italian Village's artist in residence. As plans developed, our committee quickly expanded to include a dozen members of the sponsoring organization, the American Italian Federation of the Southeast.

As a backdrop for the exhibit, local designer Jack Siciliano created a collage of vintage St. Joseph Altars from photographs of his and my family's collections. Taking a cue from the Hallmark exhibit, we preserved all the foods displayed on the altar by coating them with an acrylic spray.

St. Joseph Altar exhibit as part of the Italian Village at the 1984 Louisiana World's Fair. *Left to right,* Joseph Maselli, chairman, Italian Village; Madlyn Accardo Scalise, president, St. Lucy Society of New Orleans; Most Reverend Philip M. Hannan, archbishop of New Orleans; Sandra Scalise Juneau, secretary, St. Lucy Society of New Orleans; Reverend Monsignor Ignatius M. Roppolo.

The fair opened in May 1984, and the Italian Village became a favorite gathering spot for locals and visitors. The St. Joseph Altar exhibit proved a huge success, but by the end of the third week we noticed that our *cuccidati* and decorative breads were beginning to wilt. What we hadn't factored in was Louisiana's summertime humidity. So, every third week through the fair's end in November, all of the foods on the altar had to be freshly made and coated with acrylic spray. Despite the extra labor, it was well worth the effort, as we were gratified to receive much loving appreciation from locals and first-time visitors.

The American Italian Cultural Center Display

By the early 1990s, a renovation was underway at the Italian American Renaissance Foundation Museum and Research Library at 537 South Peters Street in New Orleans, just beside the Piazza d'Italia. Museum officials contacted me and asked me to produce a small St. Joseph Altar for permanent display. Working with the National Park Service and with funding from the Smithsonian Institution, we contracted with a Japanese food-art company in California to replicate each altar display piece in plastic. The art company requested three identical samples of each item, including decorative *cuccidati,* breads, *pignolati,* cannoli, and assorted biscotti. I explained that creating these foods was a form of folk art, that each design would be slightly different, and that no two pieces could be exactly alike, an explanation they accepted.

Over the next few weeks, I made three of each item, including cannoli shells that I stuffed with cotton to look like ricotta filling. With the help of Allison Pena, cultural anthropologist with the National Park Service, we packaged the items in cartons, sank them into six-inch-thick plastic foam, and shipped them off to California. Several months later the plastic food pieces arrived back in Louisiana, each so amazingly realistic that we had to touch them to convince ourselves they were indeed replicas.

Moving forward with the museum project, to dress the altar, I worked with a committee of helpers to assemble the linens, candelabra, silk flowers, candles, and a statue of St. Joseph. By St. Joseph's Day of 1992, the altar was blessed and open for visitors to experience it year-round.

The foundation has since changed its name to the American Italian Cultural Center. In its most recent renovation, it features a new St. Joseph Altar exhibit, which is a full-sized photo of an altar.

The Southern Food and Beverage Museum Display

Exhibit at the Southern Food and Beverage Museum.

In 2007 I was contacted by Nora Wetzel, food stylist and chef owner of the Educated Palate Catering Company. Nora is also a lifelong friend of Liz Williams, president of the National Food & Beverage Foundation. Williams was planning the opening of SoFAB, the Southern Food and Beverage Museum, in its original location inside New Orleans's Riverwalk Marketplace. One of the permanent exhibits Williams wanted to include was a St. Joseph Altar, a tradition she cherished from her family of Sicilian heritage, and I wholeheartedly agreed to help.

To replicate the delicate lacy designs of *cuccidati* and the specialty items of *pignolati,* assorted biscotti, and breads, we decided to use a salt dough which, once baked, would result in permeant replicas. Working with salt dough proved to be challenging. It was especially difficult to produce the right texture and pliability for carving, and working with the harsh mixture was particularly hard on my hands.

After many trials, we came up with a satisfactory dough. After shaping, each food piece had to be baked, then cooled before decorating and sealing. Nora created decorative breads, baskets, biscotti, and *pignolati* that she painted and glazed with a coating of shellac. For the lacy *cuccidati* designs I created, the interiors had to be carefully painted in dark brown to replicate the fig filling, then dried before coating with shellac. We finally completed each piece, had a three-tiered wooden St. Joseph Altar constructed, and stored everything at the museum to await the opening.

During the week before the opening of SoFAB, New Orleans was hosting the Thirtieth Annual Conference of IACP, the International Association of Culinary Professionals, which was attended by over two thousand culinary experts. The conference's opening reception was held outdoors in the open plaza at New Orleans's Spanish Plaza, and it showcased Louisiana food, products, and restaurants. Louisiana chef John Folse, coordinator of the event, asked me to present a St. Joseph Altar and to demonstrate the art of *cuccidati* carving. With the help of SoFAB staff, we moved everything we had gathered for the altar down to Spanish Plaza, which is along the river just downstairs from the Riverwalk Marketplace. We set up the altar and secured everything in place. What we hadn't factored in was the wind whipping off the Mississippi River, and as the night progressed, we had to tape everything down on the altar, including the statue of St. Joseph.

After the reception, the altar was moved back upstairs to the museum. The SoFAB Museum opened with great success, and on Sunday, August 17, 2008, we held the Blessing of the St. Joseph Altar, presided over by Reverend Monsignor Ignatius Roppolo. Now part of the National Food & Beverage Foundation, the exhibit is on permanent display at the Southern Food & Beverage Museum's new location at 1504 Oretha Castle Haley Boulevard in New Orleans.

A World Full of Love

I am constantly amazed by St. Joseph's way of connecting people. Several years ago, I received a small newspaper clipping in the mail announcing a St. Joseph Altar at the home of Rosie Scalise Sheraton in Rockford, Illinois. The clipping was sent to me by a friend who had been in Illinois and happened to notice our shared last name. There was no telephone number, just the date of the altar and the address. I called the local Catholic church in Rockford, inquired about contacting Rosie Scalise Sheraton, and they gave me her telephone number. I telephoned her, and we shared St. Joseph Altar stories over the phone and by email. Through the years, Rosie and I have enjoyed visiting, both at her home in Rockford and at my home in Madisonville, Louisiana.

Though we are not related, and despite sharing the same last name, Rosie and I have become family. On one occasion I prepared *cuccidati* in her home. In attendance were three generations of her family, including her parents, Martha and Carl Scalise, a nephew, and a room full of friends. I quickly realized an amazing connection—their St. Joseph Altar preparations are exactly the same as those I learned from my maternal grandmother. And in Rosie's kitchen I also felt the closeness of family. As Rosie describes the experience, "Bringing family and friends together to work in honor of St. Joseph is a wonderful gathering that is always about the love in the labor."

Aside from sharing experiences with individuals, I have been privileged to extend the St. Joseph Altar story through the media. A special taping came about in 2006 when Chef John Folse was planning for a Louisiana Public Broadcasting feature, *A Taste of Louisiana,* and he included a segment on the St. Joseph Altar tradition. I was honored when he came to my home with his production crew to film the *cuccidati*-making process. I was again honored in

2019 when WLAE-TV interviewed me about the Sicilian tradition of St. Joseph Altars for their production *The Church in the Crescent City: 300 Years of Catholicism in New Orleans.*

For me, the most gratifying St. Joseph Altar experiences have been while working with students, whose enthusiasm is always infectious. Among the many classes I have taught have been lectures and hands-on presentations to passionate enrollees of the Italians in America program led by Dr. Joseph V. Ricapito at Louisiana State University in Baton Rouge, and for the Italian studies program led by Dr. Lucia Harrison at Southeastern Louisiana University in Hammond. A series of classes I taught in 2007 at the Chef John Folse Culinary Institute of Nicholls State University in Thibodaux, Louisiana, was especially rewarding, because of the genuine interest of these future culinarians who were embracing centuries-old recipes.

Another amazing experience happened in 2012, when I was contacted by Dr. Kim Vaz-Deville, associate dean of the College of Arts and Sciences and professor of education at Xavier University of Louisiana. Dr. Vaz-Deville's goal was to offer freshman students a class on the history of the St. Joseph Altar tradition, with the hands-on experience of preparing *cuccidati* for an altar on campus that would be made by students and open to faculty, students, and visitors. In a huge auditorium, we set up a dozen round tables of eight, with a workstation for each student that included a cutting board, carving tool, ingredients for preparing the *cuccidati* dough, and a portion of fig paste. After a brief lecture and video presentation, students worked in pairs to prepare the dough. They then created their own design.

It truly was a joyful learning experience for all who attended. Dr. Vaz-Deville was thrilled that her students learned about the beloved New Orleans tradition, and that they also learned the unique skill of carving *cuccidati* shapes. The program was so successful that the St. Joseph Altar tradition continues at Xavier University, where every year a new crop of freshman students comes together on a Saturday morning to roll, cut, and carve their individual designs.

The St. Joseph Altar at Xavier University is a testament to African culture. The altar is dressed with symbolic tribal Kente cloth, embellished with handmade woven baskets, and with original student artworks from the XULA Department of Art. According to Dr. Vaz, when her students participate in

St. Joseph Altar designed by students at Xavier University of Louisiana.
Photo by Anthony "Chopper" Leone.

creating the altar, they gain an opportunity to reflect on how they are preparing themselves to be of service to others and to reflect on the special work in life they have been called to do.

I also found enthusiasm in a younger group of students at my high-school alma mater, St. Mary's Dominican in New Orleans. In 2016, I assisted the Dominican Sisters of Peace and the Alumnae Association with preparations for a St. Joseph Altar on campus that was open for visitors. Additionally, I was asked to teach a class of students about the history and symbolism of the tradition. Not only were the students attentive, but they asked questions and related their own cherished stories about family altars.

Experiencing St. Joseph Altars that are not only multigenerational, but also cross-cultural, has provided amazing opportunities for sharing the legacy of this heritage, and for learning how this tradition is embraced by all. For example, not far from my home is the Sacred Heart Church Parish in Lacombe, Louisiana. I was fortunate in 2017 to assist in preparations for their St. Joseph

Altar and was struck by the leadership of Mrs. Helen Doucette, director of their St. Joseph Altar Committee. The loving gathering of these neighbors and family members as they prepared for the altar is best described by Mrs. Doucette:

> Our St. Joseph Altar at Sacred Heart Church in Lacombe is truly a "Labor of Love." We imitate the humility of St. Joseph by begging for all the foods, which are donated by our community and are distributed within our community when we "break-down" after the Blessing of the Altar. What is unique about our St. Joseph Altar is that it represents our multi-cultural community—we are the descendants of the Choctaw, and the Spanish, French, and African Creole families who have settled here since the late 1600s. We know we are on sacred ground, for this is where Abbé Adrien Roquette established his Mission to the Choctaw Indians.

These stories reinforce the continuity of this tradition. The St. Joseph Altar custom is an old one, and to construct an altar properly requires time, planning, and dedication. But judging by the interest from art galleries, museums, social societies, the news media, churches, high schools, and universities, I am reassured that this sacred practice will endure.

Acknowledgments

With grateful appreciation for their assistance:

To the Most Reverend Gregory M. Aymond, archbishop of New Orleans, for writing the foreword and in it sharing his insightful observations on the significance of this sacred tradition.

My team at Louisiana State University Press: Cynthia LeJeune Nobles, series editor for the Southern Table, for encouragement through each step of this journey, refining each word, adjusting for correctness; and James W. Long, acquisitions editor, for bringing this story to life.

For his artistry and enduring patience, my dear friend, photographer Anthony "Chopper" Leone.

To those friends who assisted in countless ways: Celeste Shelsey Anding, Donna Bakewell, Carole Cuoco Bauer, Erin Belk, Shelly Belk, Linda Almerico Belou, Nancy Berg, Jane Ann Gumina Bergeron, Denise Parra Bostic, Arthur Bocato, Gayle Camus, Maria Bertucci Compagno, Gaylyn Reilly Danner, Barbara Jurisich Decker, Kim Vaz-Deville, Helen Doucette, Mary Evelyn Barba Doody, Judy LaCour Drez, Ronald J. Drez, Deborah Faust, Chef John Folse, Rose Margaret Fratello, Therese Juneau Fury, the Reverend Monsignor Frank J. Giroir, Paul Goethel, Virginia Grubb, Lucia G. Harrison, Elsa Hodge, Frances Drago Hymel, Jeanne Michelle Juneau, Marc Bernard Juneau, Susan Kierr, Angelina Sottile Legnon, Ann Ferrera Leonard, Steve Nuccio, Cathie McFarland, Gayle Allain Melville, Pat Milenius, Sisters of St. Joseph, Virginia Muscarello Patecek, Rosa Ricciardi, the Reverend Father Dean L. Robins, John Roppolo, Lisa Saia, Carol Bartels St. Germain, Rosie Scalise Sheridan, Sharon Winn Smetherman,

Barbara Spiegel, Linda Stanga, Mary Toti, Chef Giovanni Vancheri, Mae Galioto Webb, and Liz Williams.

For anyone whose name I have failed to include, I offer my sincere apology. After a journalist had visited my grandmother Angelina's home for interviewing and photographing the St. Joseph Altar baking in her kitchen, I became incensed when the published newspaper article failed to include her name. In her serenely devout manner, my grandmother quietly assured me, "It's okay. St. Joseph knows."

Appendix A

Litany and Rosary of St. Joseph

The following are the Litany and Rosary prayers to St. Joseph, in both Sicilian dialect and in English. In my family, the recitation and singing of this litany was a sacred part of the St. Joseph Altar tradition. I have fond memories from earliest childhood of my great-grandmother Michaela Tridico Caronna leading this beautiful prayer, as a group of elder ladies, including my grandmother Accardo, answered the prayers. The women said these prayers as a novena, repeated daily during the nine days prior to the Feast of St. Joseph, and traditionally recited them as a chanting song on the evening before the blessing of the St. Joseph Altar. Unfortunately, we have no documentation of the age of this practice.

Litania a San Giuseppi

Signuri, aviti pitati pi nuiatri,
Cristu, aviti pitati pi nuiatri,
Signuri, aviti pitati pi nuiatri,
Cristu, sintiti a nuiatri,
Cristu, sintiti gintirmenti a nuiatri.

Diu, lu Patri di Celu,)
Diu, lu Figghiu, Sarvaturi dû munnu,)

Diu, lu Spìritu Santu,) Aviti pitati pi nuiatri
La Trinnitati Santa, unu Diu,)

Santa Marìa,)
San Giuseppi,)
Proli rinumata di Dàvidi,)
Luci di patriarchi,)

Spusu dâ Matri di Diu,) Prigati pi nuiatri
Custodiu puru dâ Virginedda,)
Patri aduttivu dû Figghiu di Diu,)
Prutitturi diliggenti di Cristu,)
Capu dâ Famigghia Santa,)

Giuseppi cchiui iustu,) Prigati pi nuiatri
Giuseppi cchiui puru,)
Giuseppi cchiui prudenti,)
Giuseppi cchiui forti,)
Giuseppi cchiui uvvidenti,)
Giuseppi cchiui fidili,) Prigati pi nuiatri
Specchiu di pacenza,)
Amanti di puvirtati,)
Asempiu d'artizana,)
Gloria dâ vita dâ casa,)

Custodiu dî vìrgini,)
Sustegnu dî famigghi,)
Cunfurtanti dî disgrazziati,) Prigati pi nuiatri
Spiranza dî malatìi,)
Patronu dî murticeddi,)
Scantu dî dimoni,)
Prutitturi dâ Chesa Santa.)
Agneddu di Diu, ca nni livati li
piccati dû munnu; Sparagnàtini, O Signuri.

Agneddu di Diu, ca nni livati li piccati dû munnu;	Sintìtini gintirmenti, O Signuri.
Agneddu di Diu, ca nni livati li piccati dû munnu;	Aviti pitati pi nuiatri.

Lu fissàstivu lu Signuri dâ so casa; E Prìncipi di tuttu dâ so prupritati.

Ni Prigamu: O, Diu ca, nna vostra pruvidenza 'niffàbbili, accurdàstivu a scègghiri Giuseppi santu p'èssiri lu spusu di vostra Matri cchiui santa; Accurdati, v'impruramu, ca L'avìssimu comu lu nostru 'ntirsatturi 'n Celu, cu' Lu viniramu comu lu nostru prutitturi 'n terra: Cu' viviti e rignati munnu senza fini.

Amen.

Litany to St. Joseph

Lord, have mercy on us,
Christ, have mercy on us,
Lord, have mercy on us,
Christ, hear us,
Christ, graciously hear us.

God, the Father of Heaven,	)	
God, the Son, Redeemer of the world,	)	
God, the Holy Ghost,	)	Have mercy on us.
Holy Trinity, one God,	)	

Holy Mary,	)	
St. Joseph,	)	
Renowned offspring of David,	)	
Light of patriarchs,	)	
Spouse of the Mother of God,	)	Pray for us.
Chaste Guardian of the Virgin,	)	
Foster father of the Son of God,	)	
Diligent protector of Christ,	)	
Head of the Holy Family,	)	

Joseph most just,	)	
Joseph most chaste,	)	
Joseph most prudent,	)	
Joseph most strong,	)	
Joseph most obedient,	)	
Joseph most faithful,	)	Pray for us.
Mirror of patience,	)	
Lover of poverty,	)	
Model of artisans,	)	
Glory of home life,	)	

Guardian of virgins,	)	
Pillar of families,	)	
Solace of the wretched,	)	
Hope of the sick,	)	Pray for us.
Patron of the dying,	)	
Terror of demons,	)	
Protector of the Holy Church.	)	

Lamb of God, who takest away the sins of the world;	Spare us, O Lord.
Lamb of God, who takest away the sins of the world;	Graciously hear us, O Lord.
Lamb of God, who takest away the sins of the world;	Have mercy on us.

He made Him the Lord of His household; And prince over all His possessions.

Let us pray: O, God, Who in Thy ineffable providence didst vouchsafe to choose blessed Joseph to be the spouse of Thy most holy Mother; grant, we beseech Thee, that we may have Him for our intercessor in Heaven, whom we venerate as our protector on earth: Who livest and reignest, world without end.

Amen.

Rusariu a San Giuseppi

San Giusippuzzu chi fùstivu patri, fùstivu vìrgini comu la matri. Marìa la rosa, Giuseppi lu gigghiu, dàtini aiutu, ripari, e cunzigghiu. Prima di l'arma e poi di lu corpu, dàtini aiutu, ripari, e cummortu. Patriarca 'mmaculata di Gesù custodiu amatu. Patri e spusu di Maria, prutiggiti l'ànima mia, a lu finu di la me morti, vui sarvati la me sorti. E d'a l'ùrtima angonìa, voi sarvati l'arma mia.

PADRE NOSTRO

Padre nostrum, che sei nei cieli, sia santifico it tou nome, venga it tuo regno, sia fatta la tua volonta,' come in cielo cosi in terra. Dacci ogg il nostro pane quotidiano, e rimetti a noi nostri debiti, come noi li rimettiamo ai nostril debitori, e nonc'indurre in tentazione, ma liberaci da male.

Leader—Diu vi sarvati San Giuseppi tuttu chinu di purità.

Followers—Aiutati a li bisogn'e l'astremi nicissità. (*Repeat 10 times*)

Recite 5 decades of the Rosary. After each decade of the Rosary, repeat:

San Giusippuzzu chi fùstivu patri, fùstivu vìrgini comu la matri. Marìa la rosa, Giuseppi lu gigghiu, dàtini aiutu, ripari, e cunzigghiu. Prima di l'arma e poi di lu corpu, dàtini aiutu, ripari, e cummortu. Patriarca 'mmaculata di Gesù custodiu amatu. Patri e spusu di Maria, prutiggiti l'ànima mia, a lu finu di la me morti, vui sarvati la me sorti. E d'a l'ùrtima angonìa, voi sarvati l'arma mia.

After praying the Rosary, say:

Patriarca di San Giuseppi, furtunatu Patri di Gesù, e spusu di Marìa. Fùstivu tantu puru e furtunatu vi supplica d'una grazzia vulìa e pi ricurdari di so custatu a lu paradisu prigati pi mia. vi surfica d'una grazzia vulìa e pi ricurdari di so custatu a lu paradisu prigati pi mia. Quantu mi spera l'arma e appoi lu sciatu, assistìtimi nni l'ùrtima angonìa.

St. Joseph who was father, was a virgin like the mother; Maria the rose and Joseph the lily. Give us help, shelter, and advice. First from the soul then from the body, give us help, shelter, and satisfaction. Immaculate patriarch of Jesus blessed guardian. Father and spouse of Maria, protect my soul, until my death becomes my fate and from my last breath you save my soul.

OUR FATHER

Our Father, Who art in heaven, hallowed be Thy name; Thy kingdom come; Thy will be done on earth as it is in heaven. Give us this day our daily bread; and forgive us our trespasses as we forgive those who trespass against us; and lead us not into temptation, but deliver us from evil.

Leader—God spare St. Joseph full of purity.

Followers—Help the needs and the extreme necessities. (*Repeat 10 times*)

Recite 5 decades of the Rosary. After each decade of the Rosary, repeat:

St. Joseph who was father, was a virgin like the mother; Maria the rose and Joseph the lily. Give us help, shelter, and advice. First from the soul then from the body, give us help, shelter, and satisfaction. Immaculate patriarch of Jesus blessed guardian. Father and spouse of Maria, protect my soul, until my death becomes my fate and from my last breath you save my soul.

After praying the Rosary, say:

Patriarch of St. Joseph, fortunate Father of Jesus and spouse of Maria, was very pure and fortunate. I humbly ask for your grace, from your heart to paradise, pray for me. As much as my soul helps me and then my breath, assist me in my last breath.

Blessing Prayers of the St. Joseph Altar

This prayer is from *Viva San Giuseppe: A Guide for St. Joseph Altars,* published in 1985 by the St. Joseph Guild, Provincial House of the Sisters of St. Joseph, New Orleans.

Celebrant—O, glorious St. Joseph, we stand before this Altar with joyful and grateful hearts. We lovingly present to you the labor of our hands and the dedication of our hearts that have fashioned this Altar in your honor. We again place ourselves under your powerful protection. Help us follow your example of complete trust and faith in Divine Providence. Open our minds and hearts to love and serve the poor, the suffering and those rejected or ignored by society. As a family, teach us to love and honor each member of our families with the love and reverence you had for Jesus and Mary. As a nation, inspire in us the will and the way to live in peace with all nations of the world that in our day we can experience the fulfillment of Jesus' prayer—"Peace be to you." Grant this through Christ our Lord, who lives and reigns forever and ever.

All—Amen.

Celebrant—O, Glorious St. Joseph, through the love you bear to Jesus Christ and the glory of His name,

All—Hear our prayers and obtain our petitions.

Celebrant—Lord Jesus, bless this Altar, all this food, the candles and all those who visit it. We ask this in the name of the Father, and of the Son and of the Holy Spirit. Amen.

(As the altar is being blessed and incensed, the Litany of St. Joseph is said or a hymn is sung.)

All—Remember, O most pure spouse of the Blessed Virgin Mary, my sweet protector, St. Joseph, that no one ever had recourse to your protection or implored your aid without obtaining relief. Confiding therefore in your goodness, I come before you and humbly supplicate you. O, despise not my petitions, foster father of our Redeemer, but graciously receive them. Amen.

(*Guests are invited to visit the blessed altar and offer their own prayers to St. Joseph.*)

This blessing of the St. Joseph Altar is from St. Anselm Catholic Church Parish in Madisonville, Louisiana, Reverend Monsignor Frank J. Giror, pastor.

Priest—In the name of the Father, and of the Son, and of the Holy Spirit.

All—Amen.

Priest—May God, who has called us to be saints, be with you all.

All—And also with you.

Priest—Today we honor the memory of St. Joseph, husband of the Virgin Mary and Patron of the Universal Church. We rejoice at this table, which is a sign of God's generous Blessings and of our call to serve the poor and hungry. We pray that through the intercession of St. Joseph, we too might join the saints at the banquet of the Lord in the Heavenly Kingdom.

All—Amen.

Appendix B

Festa di San Giuseppe Menu

The following menu is from Tavola di San Giuseppe celebrations I have served to guests in my home. Inspired by family recipes for Sicilian dishes traditionally associated with St. Joseph Altars, the menu also includes dishes with Louisiana influences. Your own home celebration can be as elaborate or as simple as you prefer, celebrating la Festa di San Giuseppe with invited guests gathered around your table or open to visitors for buffet-style service.

Menu

ANTIPASTI

Caponatina

Chilled Eggplant Relish

Bruschetta

Toasted Bread Slices

I PRIMI

Melanzane al Gamberi

Shrimp-Stuffed Eggplant

PASTA

Pasta con le Sarde con Mudica

Traditional Sardine and Anise Tomato Sauce
with Currants and Pine Nuts served over Pasta and
topped with Toasted Bread Crumb

I PLATTI DI MEZZO

Froscia

Sicilian-Style Vegetable Omelet

I SECONDI

Pesce al Forno, Vino Rosso

Stuffed Redfish Baked in Tomato-Wine Sauce

I DOLCI

Cuccidati e Biscotti a la San Giuseppe

Sicilian Fig Cookies

Assorted Traditional St. Joseph's Cookies

Caffé

Italian Roast Coffee

Limoncello

Lemon Liqueur

Glossary

ABBONDANZA: Abundance, as in the abundance of blessings associated with the St. Joseph Altar tradition.

AMARETTI: Sicilian almond meringues.

ANTIPASTI: An assortment of appetizers served before the meal.

ARANCINI: Sicilian-style fried rice balls.

ARBËRESHË: An ancient Albanian culture preserved through language, religion, traditions, art, and gastronomy. Sicilian communities of Albanian refugees had been established since the fourteenth century, and many of their descendants emigrated to Louisiana in the late nineteenth century.

L'ASSOCIAZIONE PRO LOCO: The Pro Loco Association, an Italian institution dedicated to perpetuating local customs and culture.

BACCALÀ: Dried, salted codfish.

BISACQUINO: Sicilian town in the province of Palermo.

BISCOTTI: "Little biscuits," referring to a variety of traditional cookies found on St. Joseph Altars.

BLESSED BREADS: Breads blessed at the St. Joseph Altar. A small piece of blessed bread is often kept and sometimes tossed into the winds as protection from hurricanes.

BLESSING THE ALTAR: A special ceremony for blessing the food and all participants in the altar preparations.

BREAKING THE ALTAR: Packaging the foods on the altar for distribution to the community after guests have been served.

CACCAMO: Sicilian town in the province of Palermo, located on the Tyrrhenian coast.

CACIOCAVALLO: A sheep or cow's milk cheese. Literally "cheese on horseback."

CANNOLI: Sicilian confection of tube-shaped fried pastry shells filled with a creamy sweetened ricotta.

CAPONATINA: Sicilian appetizer also known as *caponata*. It's made of eggplant, celery, tomatoes, olives, capers, and pine nuts in a pungent sweet-tart sauce, and is usually served chilled.

CAPU DÂ FAMIGGHIA SANTA: Head of the Holy Family.

CARCIOFI FRITTI: Fried, fresh artichoke hearts.

CARDUNI: Cardoons, large stems of thistle plants that are related to artichokes.

CARTAS: Sicilian confections of wheel-shaped pastry dough fried and dipped in honey.

CASSATEDI: Fried, sweetened ricotta-filled pastries.

CECIDA: Chickpeas.

CEFALU: Sicilian town in the province of Palermo, located on the Tyrrhenian coast.

CHIUSA SCLAFANI: Sicilian town in the province of Palermo.

CICEROTTI: Fried dessert ravioli filled with a paste of chestnuts or chickpeas.

CONTESSA ENTELLINA: Sicilian town in the province of Palermo.

CORLEONE: Sicilian town in the province of Palermo.

crispelle di san giuseppe: Sweet fried rice balls.

cuccia: St. Lucy's Feast Day specialty, a sweet custard of whole-wheat berries cooked with honey.

cuccidati: Sicilian fig cookies, small bite-sized cookies or large symbolic shapes found on St. Joseph Altars.

cucuzza: A long, tubular light-green squash.

cugina: Female cousin.

dalla nonna alla figlia: From grandmother to daughter.

feeding of the saints: The ritual meal traditionally served after the Blessing of the Altar to those portraying the Holy Family and other saints.

la festa di san giuseppe: Feast of St. Joseph.

froscia: Sicilian-style vegetable omelet.

general garibaldi: Giuseppe Maria Garibaldi (1807–1882): Italian general and nationalist who contributed to Italian unification and the creation of the Kingdom of Italy.

gesù bambino: Baby Jesus.

gesù, maria, e san giuseppe: Jesus, Mary, and St. Joseph.

gibellina: Sicilian town in the province of Trapani.

iacp: International Association of Culinary Professionals, a US-based not-for-profit professional association that fosters culinary education and communication.

king cake: A circular cake celebrating Twelfth Night or King's Day, the official beginning of the Mardi Gras season. Anyone finding the replica of the Baby Jesus in their slice of cake is required, in remembrance of the visit of the Magi, to provide a king cake for the next party, thus perpetuating a round of parties throughout the Mardi Gras season.

LABOR OF LOVE: Work done for pleasure, not for profit. Described in the Epistle of St. Paul, 1 Thessalonians 1:3: "Remembering without ceasing your work of faith, and labour of love."

LIMONCELLO: Lemon liqueur.

LITANIA A SAN GIUSEPPE: Litany of St. Joseph. The ancient chanting prayer recited in Sicilian dialect by the faithful on the night before St. Joseph's Day.

LUCKY BEANS: Roasted, dried fava beans that are blessed and kept as mementos of a St. Joseph Altar celebration. Because fava beans were the sustaining crop following a great famine in Sicily, they became the symbol of abundance and hope.

LUNDI GRAS: Fat Monday, the day proceeding Mardi Gras, Fat Tuesday.

MAKING THE ALTAR: Assembling a crew of workers, gathering donations, scheduling baking dates, and setting up the St. Joseph Altar.

MAKING THE NINE ALTARS: Novena promise for visiting nine St. Joseph Altars.

***MUDICA*:** Sicilian-style seasoned bread crumbs, said to represent the carpenter's "sawdust" of St. Joseph. Served over pasta at the St. Joseph Day meal.

NONNA: Grandmother.

NOVENA: Prayer in nine parts, or recited over nine successive days.

OCCHI DI SANTA LUCIA: "Eyes of St. Lucy," depicted in pastry to represent the martyrdom of St. Lucy.

OSTENSORIUM: Also known as the monstrance, the vessel used in adoration of the consecrated Eucharist during Benediction of the Blessed Sacrament.

PALAZZO ADRIANO: Sicilian town in the province of Palermo.

PALERMO: Capital city of the island of Sicily.

PASTA CON LE SARDE: Traditional dish of the St. Joseph's Day feast. A Sicilian-style tomato sauce that combines the flavors of sardines, currants, and pine nuts, and served over an anise-infused pasta.

PAUL OF TARSUS: The Apostle St. Paul, born in Cilicia, now Turkey, died in Rome around the year AD 64.

PIANA DEI GRECI: Sicilian town, now called *Piana degli* Albanesi, in the province of Palermo.

PIGNOCCATA: Sicilian confection of sugared and honey-coated fried pastry mounds.

PIGNOLATI: Sicilian confection of fried pastry that is sugared and shaped into mounds to resemble pine cones.

PLAQUEMINES PARISH: A Louisiana parish (county) located south of New Orleans, noted for its citrus crop, particularly oranges.

POGGIOREALE: Sicilian town in the province of Trapani.

LA PROTEZIONE DELLA FAMIGLIA SANTA: The Protector of the Holy Family, St. Joseph.

PUPA CU L'OVA: "Puppet with eggs." Nonedible replicas of chickens fashioned in dough baked over a hard-cooked egg. Symbol of spring, rebirth, and hope.

ROCCAMENA: Sicilian town in the province of Palermo.

RICOTTA: Milk that has been recooked to separate the curds from the whey, which creates a soft mild-flavored cream.

RICOTTA SALATA: Salted ricotta.

RISOTTO: Northern Italian specialty of Arborio. Made from a short-grain rice which, when cooked with broth, creates a creamy consistency.

RUSARIU A SAN GIUSEPPE: Rosary of St. Joseph, usually recited on the evening before St. Joseph's feast day.

ST. JOSEPH ALTAR: A display of specialty foods in honor of St. Joseph, usually set in three tiers to symbolize the Holy Family: Jesus, Mary, and Joseph. The altars can be as simple or elaborate as the creativity of those preparing them. No two St. Joseph Altars are ever alike; each is the collective artistry of individual artisans.

ST. JOSEPH ALTAR SAINTS: Individuals, family, or community members selected to represent the Holy Family of Jesus, Mary, and Joseph. The group may include any number of additional saints.

ST. JOSEPH LILY: Red-and-white-striped amaryllis frequently displayed on St. Joseph Altars.

ST. JOSEPH TABLE: A smaller version of the St. Joseph Altar, usually prepared for family at home.

SALAPARUTA: Sicilian town in the province of Trapani.

SAMBUCA: Sicilian town in the province of Agrigento.

SAN GIUSEPPE: St. Joseph, spouse of Mary, the mother of Jesus. In 1870 Pope Pius IX declared St. Joseph the Patron of the Universal Church.

SANTA LUCIA: St. Lucy, the virgin martyr from Syracuse, Sicily. Since early Christianity, her feast day has been commemorated on December 13.

SCARDELLINI: Brittle-textured, Sicilian cookies prepared in commemoration of All Souls Day, celebrated on November 2. Also known as *ossa di morto,* bones of the dead.

SCHIACCIATA: Rustic, Sicilian-style pan bread.

SFINGE DI SAN GIUSEPPE: St. Joseph's Day pastry filled with sweetened ricotta cream.

SFINGIONI: Rustic, Sicilian-style pan bread.

SICILIA: Sicily.

SOUTHERN FOOD & BEVERAGE MUSEUM (SOFAB): A culinary museum in New Orleans. Part of the National Food & Beverage Foundation.

SQUARTUCCIATI: Elaborate Sicilian cutwork designs for fig-filled pastries. Literally, "lace making."

LA TAVOLA DI SAN GIUSEPPE: The Table of St. Joseph, usually a family St. Joseph Altar held at home.

TERMINI: Sicilian town in the province of Palermo.

TORRONE SICILIANO: Sicilian almond brittle.

TRABIA: Sicilian town in the province of Palermo.

TRAPANI: Sicilian city, capital of the province of Trapani.

TUPA-TUPA: "Knock-Knock" is the ceremony that reenacts the Bethlehem story, with Joseph leading Mary to find shelter for the birth of Jesus. Those portraying the saints knock at three doors until they are welcomed into the St. Joseph Altar feast that has been prepared for them.

USTICA: Sicilian island in the Tyrrhenian Sea.

Recipe Index